WHERE
THE WRITER
MEETS
THE ROAD

WHERE THE WRITER MEETS THE ROAD

A COLLECTION OF ARTICLES, BROADCAST INTROS, AND PROFILES

SAM POSEY

FOREWORD BY DAVID HOBBS

DAVID BULL PUBLISHING

Library of Congress Control Number: 2014956448

ISBN: 978 1 935007 27 2

David Bull Publishing, logo, and colophon are trademarks of David Bull Publishing, Inc.

Book and cover design: Tom Morgan, Blue Design, Portland, Maine

Printed in the United States

10 9 8 7 6 5 4 3 2 1

David Bull Publishing
4250 East Camelback Road
Suite K150
Phoenix, AZ 85018

602-852-9500
602-852-9503 (fax)

www.bullpublishing.com

To Skip Barber and Bill Warner for their extreme kindness,
which has brought such joy to my family and me.

CONTENTS

A rare shot from the archives. David is ahead as we plunge down the Corkscrew at Laguna Seca. Hobbs is driving the McLaren in which he would win the 1971 F5000 championship. I would be second in my Surtees.

Foreword

DAVID HOBBS—TUESDAY, JULY 22, 2014

Sam and I first met in 1969, when John Surtees sent me over to the big colony to take part in the second half of the FA Championship, as it was known then. My first race at Road America was not a roaring success. However, very soon after things began to take off, and I'm afraid I rather rained on Sam's parade. At Lime Rock, Sam's beloved home track, I came in second behind another Englishman, Peter Gethin, and worse was to come. Winning the next three races—losing the championship by one point, having only done six races, but still well ahead of Sam—was too much. Sam had always been vociferous, but now he turned into "Motormouth."

Coming from England, where we are supposed to be very understated, polite, and generally self-deprecating, Sam came as a bit of a shock. He was having trouble beating me on the track, and was determined to trump me in the press. My parents were Australian, so I didn't suffer from the English malaise, and was not backward in coming forward, so I joined in.

This seemed to be the birth—fortunately for me, and Sam, too, I suspect—of a complete life change. For the next three years the verbal and written exchanges between Sam and me became the linchpin in the promotion of the newly named "L&M F5000 Championship." Creating publicity was a difficult task in those pre-racing TV days. Rod Campbell, principal of the PR company that L&M employed to promote the series, almost exclusively used Sam and me across the country, with newspapers and in radio and TV stations. We kept up our constant denigration of each other even as our friendship and appreciation of each other continued to grow.

I have to acknowledge, however, that his fertile imagination certainly brought him out on top. I'm convinced these exchanges became our passport to our second careers. Sam retired from racing in the mid-1980s; the end of his driving overlapped with his television career. He joined ABC, where he became a mainstay in the Indy 500 broadcast for more than two decades. During this time the TV ratings for the race were at their highest. In 1976 I joined CBS, and continued to race until 1990.

In 1975, Sam wrote his first book, *The Mudge Pond Express*, an early memoir of his life and racing up to that point. The book illustrated his very competitive nature starting as a small boy, and particularly with his closest friend, John Whitman, building racing karts and race tracks on the family estate. It's a fascinating insight into his early life, and unlike any other race book found in the sports section of the library. I think it's a very good read.

Sam came from a very different background than mine. He went to the best schools, where his intellect and artistic talents soon became evident, finishing his education at the very prestigious Rhode Island School of Design. During his childhood Sam became fascinated by railway trains, both real and model. As a boy he would travel by train from New York City to the family vacation spot at Boca Grande, Florida. It was a long journey for a small boy, but it gave him plenty of time to thoroughly study his mode of transport. Sam now has at his home one of the finest model railroads in existence. This love of model trains, being well-known among the model train fraternity, led to a commission to write his second book, *Playing with Trains*. This publication has been a true bestseller, and is now in its umpteenth reprinting.

I'm not sure why Sam ever wanted to race, with all this artistic intellect buzzing around his brain. But race he did, and successfully enough to become a colorful figure in the world of motor racing. But his art, his architecture, his eloquent words, and elegant writing have made him famous.

In 1968 he started to write for *Road & Track*. This magazine has gone through a tremendous upheaval over the years. Ownership, management, editorial staff, and location have all profoundly changed.

The only constant is that Sam's name remains on the masthead, where it has been since that first article appeared in 1968.

In this book you will read a selection of those articles. Sam's appraisals and perspectives on many of our best-known drivers—obviously, I will not be included—along with some film scripts make for interesting reading. Of special note are the essays that Sam has written for multiple TV channels, including "Posey's Perspective." These are among the most eagerly awaited segments featured in practically every US televised Formula One grand prix since 1996. These popular essays are also a feature of the classic sports-car races, including the Le Mans 24 Hours, in which Sam came in a lucky and very distant third in 1971—although somehow, with the aid of smoke and mirrors, I suspect, he did win the Sebring 12 Hours.

I fully expect this collection of Sam's articles, appraisals, and essays to be equally well received. Thousands of Formula One TV viewers will love to read again his fascinating perspectives on teams, drivers, and the state of F1. And his earlier articles in *Road & Track* will no doubt stir many nostalgic memories.

Well done, Sam; you trumped me . . . again.

Acknowledgments

My thanks to Archie Urciuoli—this book was his idea.

So few people were involved in putting it together, it must be some sort of record.

In the East, Shari Marks did . . . everything. No Shari, no book. My son John came up with the title and proofread the manuscript. Chuck Queener was a sort of godfather.

In the West, publisher David Bull, designer Tom Morgan, and copyeditor Melissa Hayes managed the final assembly.

I admire great photographers, and you will find some of their work in these pages. Obviously, my favorite is my wife, Ellen, who uses her maiden name—Griesedieck—as the photo credit for many of the shots included here.

As for the shopworn phrase, "A picture is worth a thousand words," I believe certain pictures of racing cars express something that no number of words can. I know I have felt their power.

Nearly all of the cars I drove were sold at the end of the season (at the time, a year-old racing car seemed next to worthless). I never kept track of where they went, and most of them just seemed to vanish. Of course, now the cars are worth a fortune, and pictures are the only connection I have with them. Racing cars may be inanimate objects, but they were created and maintained by men I liked and admired, and these pictures help me to remember them, too.

Thank you to photographers: John Atchley, Tom Blagden, Ellen Griesedieck, Edwin Ingalls, Mary Moore, Dos Pierson, John Poland, and Ronald Suter. And also thanks to LAT and the Sam Posey Collection.

First, you have to show up.
Next, you have to finish.
Only then can you think of winning.

Bruce McLaren

Introduction

The first time I wrote anything about racing was in the pressroom at Bridgehampton. Al Bochroch, a PR man for DuPont, asked me to write a couple of paragraphs for a press release. "Just describe the part of the track you found the most difficult," he said, giving me ten minutes.

I had just finished qualifying, and my impressions were still vivid. I chose the notorious fifth-gear double-apex downhill, and had a tough time when I tried to describe the layers of sensation and emotion that I felt had to be included. It was dark by the time I finished. Al spread the word that I could write as well as drive, and it led to jobs with several magazines. Eventually I settled in with *Road & Track*. Starting in 1968, I have written two or three articles a year for them, and the variety of subject matter is thanks to editors Tom Bryant, Matt DeLorenzo, and Larry Webster, each of whom has given me the opportunity to pursue ideas that were well off the beaten path. These articles are generally the longest pieces in this collection. Road-test a steam locomotive; why not? Criticize Porsche amid all the hoopla of the company's 50th anniversary? Go for it.

The second type of writing in this book is known in the TV world as a "tease"; it's that 90-second artsy beginning to every sports show. I wrote my first teases when I was working at ABC, heavily influenced by the greatest tease-writer of all, Jim McKay. His iconic "the thrill of victory, the agony of defeat," written for the first-ever Wide World of Sports, used simple words to create complex emotions. When Jim began to cut back his schedule, I inherited the sort of show that was his trademark—the Iditarod, the Ironman, the Tour de France, the Baja 1000—and I began developing my own style.

When you're writing a tease, the primary objective is to set up the pictures. But there's always the possibility of venturing into McKay territory, to go for something that will really grip your audience. Here your editor is critical, and I've been lucky to work with Justin Kircher on our travels from Speedvision to Fox Sports, and now NBC, and to have bosses like Frank Wilson and Rich O'Connor. This is high-stakes stuff; our audience is in the millions, and if we can move people—as we did with our piece about Mark Webber leaving F1—we feel we've really contributed to the show. .

The third element is the driver profiles. Each year the Road Racing Drivers Club honors a driver, and I write a tribute that my friend Tom Davey illustrates with slides and video. The honorees—Dan Gurney, Parnelli Jones, and four others—are heroes to me, which makes writing about them particularly enjoyable.

Articles, teases, and profiles—three different kinds of writing, three styles that emerged from different requirements—a sort of verbal version of "Form follows function."

Looked at one way, this book is an autobiography, the sequel to *The Mudge Pond Express*, which was published in 1976, roughly halfway through my career as a driver. ("Fast Company" is the story of my last race.) Neither book has much in it about my life as a designer and painter. Briefly, I have designed houses (about 45), a school, and, with my brother David Moore, the start/finish tower at Lime Rock. As for painting, I went to the Rhode Island School of Design, and I've been a painter all my life. In the last few years, I've concentrated on the human figure—nudes—and with models coming and going, my studio is an exciting place. And then there's my model train layout . . . A great life? You bet, and I hope reading about it here lets me share it with you.

*If Sam, the very fast and capable racing driver, writes a book,
I want to read it. He has a way with words just as he did
with a steering wheel and the gas pedal. With a style all his
own, and surprising insights, Sam can crawl into the helmet
of a driver and tell you what the driver experiences hurtling
toward the green flag at the Indy 500. With equal ease he
can rhapsodize like a poet on the golden buildings flanking
the Monaco circuit. When it comes to communicating what
motor racing is all about, nobody does it better!*

—Dan Gurney

*Over the years, I've gotten to know and respect Sam Posey
not only as a driver, but as a gifted storyteller with incredible
insight into the sport we both love. His writing is so vivid, it
makes you understand what it feels like behind the wheel of
a race car riding along with him in the cockpit. His eloquent
descriptions of man, machine, and race venues are unparal-
leled. To this day, I eagerly look forward to Sam's finely
crafted and colorful Formula One race introductions, which
accelerate the excitement building up to the start.*

—Mario Andretti

My 300SL has played a larger part in my life than any other car. When I bought it, I didn't have much going for me. I was 40 pounds overweight, and my grades were terrible. Owning the SL (the gullwing doors!) gave me some self-esteem, and from there on things got progressively brighter. I was too young to have a license, but I lived on a farm, and out there in the fields, I cut big, broad arcs through the alfalfa in the style of today's drifters. Although I didn't realize it then, the field driving—with its low grip—gave me a great head start for racing itself, where the car is always balanced on the thin edge of control.

The SL and Me
ROAD & TRACK, MAY 2010

first spotted the SL in a local showroom where they often had exotic cars on display. It was 1958, the SL was 4, and I was 14. I wanted it desperately. I was fanatical about becoming a racing driver, and here was a connection with Mercedes-Benz and all the mythology surrounding its invincible racing team. In my fevered brain, I saw ownership of the SL conferring some of the Mercedes legend on me.

The convertible SLs were just coming out—with real doors—and the Gullwing was yesterday's news, for sale at $2,500. I couldn't buy it without my mother's blessing, and, of course, there was the matter of having to borrow the money. She was hesitant. She grasped what a bargain it was, but worried that a Mercedes-Benz 300SL was too ostentatious for a young kid still in high school.

She wasn't concerned by how fast it was; on a test drive along an unpatrolled back road with her on board, I took it up to 120, and she could see that I was right at home. We lived on a farm, and with her encouragement, I had been driving for years in an assortment of farm vehicles and a '49 Ford. Although I was only 14, with two years to go before I could get my license, she understood that we were talking about something other than basic transportation. All she had to go on were intangibles, so she came up with one of her own: She said that my father, who had been killed in World War II, would have let me have it if he were alive—that he had a kind of go-for-it attitude. So, on the biggest day of my life, the SL became mine.

Getting into it called for a specific sequence of movements. First, you sat on the broad, red-leather sill. (The sills concealed the small-diameter tubes of the lightweight space-frame chassis. For torsional rigidity, the frame needed to occupy the space where a door would ordinarily have been, which left the designers no choice but to have the doors swing up.) Next, you released the catch on the hinged steering wheel (pivoting the bottom of the wheel forward) and swung your legs in. Then you dropped into the bucket seat. Finally, you reached up for the door handle and pulled the door down. *Thunk.*

Eye-eee—fuel pump on. Choke—pulled out. Then turn the absurdly small key, which looked too small to unlock a briefcase. I'd head for the fields and farm roads. For weeks that first summer, I practiced my heel-and-toe technique. I tore up fields as I learned to drift, stopping now and then to clear the alfalfa out of the radiator. There were several blind turns around the barns, and I was lucky that I never encountered a Farmall tractor coming the other way.

Occasionally I'd go for a late-night run on public roads. Magazines had touted the SL as being good for 160 mph, but the most I ever saw was 145 . . . with the car hard to hold in a straight line along the uneven crown of the road. But what the SL did was less important to me than how I reacted. Did I have the right stuff? I was convinced I did, and I ached to prove it in races.

I was an avid student of the sport and knew that the Gullwings had earned themselves a place in history through their racing successes, which included victories at Le Mans and the Carrera Panamericana. But it was the SL's 1,000 miles on the roads of Italy during the 1955 Mille Miglia that meant the most to me. In the same race that Stirling Moss drove a Mercedes-Benz SLR to victory, John Fitch was having the drive of his life, bringing a stock 300SL home fifth overall, and winning the GT class. And John Fitch was a neighbor. Although he lived just 10 miles away, I'd never had the nerve to try to meet him. But owning the SL made things different, emboldening me to ask him for a lesson.

He agreed, and we met at Lime Rock. I viewed the lesson as merely a pretext to tear around the track, showing the great John Fitch what I could do. When I arrived, I saw that he had used some cones to lay out a slalom course on the main straight. A slalom! That wasn't what I had in mind at all. He took the car for a run through the cones.

"This won't work," he said, raising the door. "Your shocks are shot." The miles in the fields had pounded them to mush. But he let me make a few laps of the track, and something convinced him that I was quite serious about racing. After that, he became—and still is—a sort of informal mentor.

A couple of years later, I was old enough, at last, to begin racing. In a sense, at that moment the SL's mission was accomplished: It had been a physical embodiment of my desire to race, then a tool for learning some of the mechanics of driving fast, and finally a connection to John Fitch. I might have considered selling it, but the beauty of living on a farm is that space can always be found somewhere. Once I was racing full-time, the SL sat up on blocks in one of the barns.

The next time I remember driving it was in June 1971, on a rare weekend home between races. Tony Adamowicz and I had just finished third at Le Mans in a NART Ferrari, I was dumbfounding David Hobbs with my speed in F5000, and I was in love with Ellen, my wife to be. In short, life was good.

Jim Haynes, the general manager of Lime Rock and one of the earliest proponents of vintage racing, suggested we attend the hillclimb at Mount Equinox, Vermont. My mom liked the idea and said she'd go, so down off the blocks came the SL, and up we went to Vermont.

We had rooms in the hotel at the top of the mountain, and Jim met us for supper. "Everything's set," he said, and he told me what class I was in and who the opposition was. The opposition! I had been thinking of the event as a demonstration, a tour up the hill, not a race. I had never raced the SL, and I couldn't settle for less than John Fitch would—winning.

"I need to learn the course," I said to Jim, but then I realized I didn't have enough gas.

"Here," Jim said, handing me some keys. "My 240Z has a full tank." In the dark, I made five or six runs up the mountain, trying to identify the critical sections. In the morning, I drove the SL down the mountain to the starting line. The early SLs, like mine, have a notorious swing-axle rear suspension that calls for a delicate touch, especially in fast corners. But Mount Equinox was mostly hairpins, and to get through them I planned to downshift into second, turn, let the rear end get loose, floor it at the apex, and exit in a smooth slide and a crowd-pleasing touch of opposite lock.

By pure chance the gearing for the straights was perfect; it was as if the car had been designed expressly for Mount Equinox. We won our class. The trophy: four glass goblets hand-painted with pictures of geese, whose outstretched wings echoed the doors of the car.

SLs were mentioned in almost everyone's list of the top 10 cars they'd like to own, and in the early 1970s they began to creep up in value. At first, I paid no attention; I thought it was just a passing fad. To me, our car's real value was sentimental. When my son John was born in 1982, my wife Ellen and I brought him home from the hospital in it—his first ride. We soon found out that a surefire way to get him to sleep was to take him out in the car, so the SL saw plenty of action that summer, rumbling along back roads in the heat and darkness.

The car was aging, however. One winter, mice built a home in the engine bay. The rubber seals around the windows began to crack. The headliner sagged. But the magic was still there. The body shape, designed by engineers, had remained fresh and original through several generations. Its history—how it was built as a statement by Mercedes to show that the company was rising from the ashes of war—demanded respect. I asked Bob Akin to do a modest restoration, and he in turn took some of the vitals to Paul Russell, the best 300SL restorer in the business. So the SL visited the Fountain of Youth and came back looking much the same, but acting with an assurance I had forgotten it had.

Shortly after its return, someone offered me the kind of money it takes to buy a house. I had promised the car to John and had no intention of selling it, but that offer, and the numbers floating around at auctions, made me see the car in a different light. Obviously, the days of storming through the fields were over. And . . . gotta check that insurance. Showing the car to visitors brought expressions of reverence. A friend, Don Breslauer, asked if he could do regular maintenance, as if the SL had become an elderly gentleman who needed someone to keep his shoes polished.

A few days ago, John took me out for a ride, and I realized I had never been a passenger in the car. He drove with the same verve and confidence that I had had when my mom and I took it for that test drive so long ago. It was a day in early fall, with the light coming in low and turning the trees into lanterns of gold and amber. In the car, the red leather glowed and the headliner was the color of wheat. Shadows flickered across the long hood. Amid all the sound and fury of the shifting, I realized the SL—which in its day was the fastest production car in the world, a car the road testers described as having "neck-snapping acceleration"—is, by modern standards, slow. Its inline-6 puts out 190 bhp at 6,000 rpm. Zero to 60 is about 7.2 seconds—performance on a par with dozens of mid-price imports.

It's over 50 years old; of course, we expect newer cars to have more raw performance just as we expect today's athletes to set new records. But there's a subjective area measured in emotion and significance, and here the SL stands out as a great car—not only of its time, but of today—and tomorrow. Masterpieces happen. Vitruvius would have said it had Firmness, Commodity, Delight . . . and gullwing doors.

As John and I rode along the other day, we wanted to go on forever, maybe even for 1,000 miles.

My uncle Teddy (pictured here in his 70s) with the machine that, as a boy, I wanted so much to drive.

The wind wagon was the creation of my uncle Ted Jameson, who was known behind his back as Crazy Teddy. This article was one of R & T's April Fools road tests, and it was made possible by Jeff Lane, who bought the Wagon at my uncle's estate sale, got it running, and let me drive it on a private track outside of Nashville.

The article was pure R & T for that period—an absurd vehicle taken seriously.

Wind Wagon
ROAD & TRACK, APRIL 2004

The Wind Wagon was the creation of my uncle Teddy. At the age of 16, infatuated with the idea of becoming a pilot, he had desperately wanted to buy, or build, a plane. His parents said no. It was 1929, and he was away at school, in Tucson, Arizona. Permission was granted, however, to construct a motorized land vehicle, so my uncle set out to create a device as close to a plane as he could get. He painted it silver, like Charles Lindbergh's *Spirit of St. Louis,* which had made its famous flight just two years before. The starting procedure mimicked aviation practice of the time: Your mechanic spun the propeller, by hand. The engine (an air-cooled V-twin Harley-Davidson) sounded like a plane's, and the prop blew wind in your face, calling for goggles and a leather flying helmet. Like most early aircraft, the Wind Wagon projected an aura of danger, and Teddy added a second seat so that his daring and bravery could be witnessed firsthand. Although it lacked torque and was slow to accelerate, its top speed, clocked on a flat Arizona highway, was 70 mph. The Wind Wagon did everything but take off.

When Teddy left school, his strange contraption was shipped back to our family's farm in Connecticut. Frustrated by its sluggish performance on the dirt roads, he waited for winter, when he took it down to a nearby lake and ran it on the ice. He persuaded his younger sister—my mother—to crouch on the rudimentary back seat, providing ballast, and then he blasted back and forth, the freezing prop wash numbing his face. When it was time to go home, Teddy tackled the steep road at full revs, but his machine barely inched along, and he soon gave up and went on to the house for hot chocolate. My mother and a friend were left to haul the machine the rest of the way.

Teddy never ran the Wind Wagon again. It was put in the storeroom of our old carriage house. The storeroom was like a cloister, shut off from the rest of the world. Light filtered through windows high in the walls, the air was still and cool, pigeons cooed in a distant cupola. In addition to the Wind Wagon, the room was crowded with other objects of my uncle's abandoned passions: a half-dozen crates containing motorcycle parts, two sailing canoes (you could smell their furled canvas sails), a large searchlight, a player piano, and a hydroplane copied from a design by Gar Wood.

I would climb aboard the Wind Wagon, settle into the seat (olive-drab velvet, possibly from a movie theater), and pretend to steer, feeling the cool, thick rim of the wheel in my hands and aching to be out on the ice, feeling the wind and noise and speed. Later, in my racing years, I would come to regard the cars I drove merely as tools of the trade, some better than others, but when I was six, the Wind Wagon exerted such a pull on my imagination that it might as well have been alive.

Teddy created the Wind Wagon because he yearned to fly (and when his chance came, he made the most of it, becoming a hero in World War II), but it also provided a preview of his obsession with anything mechanical. Fueled by a hefty inheritance, he amassed a collection of marvelous, quirky things, such as a 1919 Ford Model T "snowmobile" (skis at the front, four wheels at the back), early Indian motorcycles, exotic-looking fire trucks, a Grumman Widgeon, and a Dutch canal boat. In England, he commissioned functioning scale-model locomotives and traction engines. He rarely bought anything that someone else had restored, preferring to have it done his own way. *Hemmings* called him a "committed vehicle preservationist who commanded respect among some of the world's most serious collectors and historians," but to my family he was "Crazy Teddy," who hardly ever finished his projects and was always short of cash.

Teddy died two years ago, at the age of 89, and his collection was auctioned off. Jeff and Susan Lane of the Lane Motor Museum in Nashville, Tennessee, bought the Wind Wagon, and soon afterward called me to ask if I would like to drive it. Of course I said yes, but I wondered if they could get it running; after all, more than 70 years had elapsed since it went into storage. The Lanes got to work, modifying the ignition by installing a Citroën 2CV coil and a small battery, reconditioning the propeller (amazingly, the original manufacturer was still in business), and mounting new tires. I borrowed Teddy's leather flying helmet from my brother Nick and bought a ticket to Nashville.

A private race track, somewhere in western Tennessee. A cold, clear morning. The Wind Wagon had been trailered out, wrapped in a tarp. Now the tarp was off. *R & T*'s ace lensman Joe Rusz had his cameras warmed up, and road test editor Patrick Hong was unpacking the instruments that would measure the Wagon's performance. Since performance is relative, I wondered what exactly we were going to compare the Wagon to. A small plane? A motorcycle? The Lanes—who are well versed in strange machines—pointed out its close resemblance to a 1927 Leyat Helica, a French car with a propeller (see *R & T* photo, page 85, February 2004). I was reminded of one of Leonardo da Vinci's 16th-century siege machines—part catapult, part battering ram, part flying machine. Comedian Bill Dana (who attended the test) called it a giant salami slicer.

Seen from above, the main frame is a triangle, made of 2-inch angle iron, with an 18-inch-diameter wheel at each corner. (Tire size is 4.50 x 18.) Fastened to the frame is a 3/8-inch plywood floor. The torsional rigidity of this assembly is roughly that of a Persian rug. The superstructure supporting the engine is made of 1¼-inch angle iron and, unlike the frame, it is triangulated by cross bracing. Some of the pieces have been laboriously filed to a knife edge, presumably Teddy's idea of reducing aerodynamic drag. Another time-consuming aero touch: cutting and soldering a pair of tin cans to form the pointed ends of the combination gas and oil tank at the very top of the superstructure.

So far, these are the design decisions you might expect from an overeager 16-year-old. But when it comes to the way the engine is fitted to the frame, the level of sophistication suddenly gets much higher, suggesting that my uncle may have had some help. The engine is a stressed member positioned slightly off center (to the right, looking from the front), which would counteract the modest torque (the prop rotates counterclockwise). Everything is bolted, not welded, together, and there are no extra holes—which meant it had to have been carefully planned.

As for the suspension, there isn't any. A solid axle is fastened to the front of the frame, while at the back the rear half of a motorcycle has been grafted on, crudely, with the original chain sprocket (now useless) left in place. The extraneous sprocket and the cockeyed mounting of a round Goodyear Tire sign (the passenger's seatback) reflect my uncle's immaturity at the time of the Wind Wagon's construction, but he would soon become a manic perfectionist who delighted in spotting flaws in the work of even the best craftsmen.

Whuuuh, whuuuh. Greg Coston, the museum's chief restorer, was turning the prop. I was sitting in the driver's seat with the ignition on, the spark advance set, the hand throttle cracked open, and my foot firmly on the Wind Wagon's only pedal, the brake. The cockpit is a triumph of minimalism: The driver isn't troubled by gauges or switches. Views out are excellent in all directions—except, of course, forward. The machine's one amenity, air-conditioning, is world-class. To the right of the driver's seat is a tank containing three quarts of oil. Pumped, by hand, every minute or so, this oil provides lubrication for the rod bearings and crankshaft.

Now Greg was reaching again for the prop. *Whuuuh, Whuuuh . . . WABBADA WABBADA BWAM! WABBADA WABBADA . . .* The prop was whirling and Jeff Lane was giving me the thumbs-up. I retarded the spark, opened the throttle, released the brake . . . and I was moving. First impression: wind tearing at my face, the frame vibrating, a deafening racket. For a split second, amid all this sound and fury, I thought I might lose control. Then I glanced down at the road and saw that we were just creeping along. A butler, walking alongside, could have served me tea.

The 1213cc Harley-Davidson, at its 2,500 rpm maximum, puts out about 20 horsepower. The Wind Wagon weighs 505 pounds (over 700 with me aboard). These are not high-performance numbers, and yet the impression of acceleration was glorious. As we gathered speed, surging from 0 to 30 in 14.6 seconds, it was as if the prop had been a slipping clutch that was beginning to bite. The end of the straight approached in a hurry. The track was smooth, but thanks to the flexing of the frame the Wind Wagon was porpoising like an early ground-effect racer. I closed the throttle, foolishly expecting that, as in a car, the engine compression would provide some braking force. Instead, we just freewheeled along. For a fleeting moment I thought that after the Wind Wagon had endured 70 years in storage, I was about to wreck it at the first turn I came to. I pushed on the brake—hard.

The brake pedal is connected to a rod that runs down the right side of the frame. The rod attaches to a metal band, which tightens around the wheel hub. Patrick Hong would measure the stopping force as 0.25g (versus 1.0g for the new BMW 545i). I was coming into the turn far faster than I would have liked. Before the test, I had feared tipping over. The lateral cornering load acting on the weight of the engine and fuel tank high in the superstructure (the prop's centerline is a whopping 53 inches above the ground), plus the three-wheeled layout, looked like a formula for a flip. As far as I knew, Teddy had never attempted any serious cornering—and the dirt roads and ice would have offered little grip in any case. So this was something new for the old Wagon, and I leaned into the turn as far as I could, shifting my weight like John Surtees and hoping for the best.

Not to worry. We scooted through without a hint of instability. As the laps went by, I pushed harder in the turns, sometimes even riding the curbs, and all I felt was a bit of understeer. Teddy's fantasy airplane was being reborn as a road racer! I began to think maybe there could be a class. Fit wider tires, of course, and lower the center of gravity by dropping the engine a couple of feet, so the prop just misses the ground. Suddenly, it's Indy 2008, and 33 Wind Wagons are lined up on the front straight. The PA crackles: "Gentlemen: Start your salami slicers!"

We put 30 miles on the Wind Wagon that day, probably doubling its total mileage. But this is only the beginning. Jeff plans to run it regularly at the museum, where he expects it will be a big hit with the kids. For "Crazy Teddy's" wacky and wonderful machine, the long wait is over.

Introduction for Road Racing Drivers Club Honoree: Mario Andretti

LONG BEACH, CALIFORNIA, APRIL 10, 2014

The lights flash in your rearview mirror, and moments later the cop is leaning in your window. "Who do think you are— Mario Andretti?" he says.

It's a rhetorical question, of course; neither you nor the cop actually knows Mario, but his name is a kind of shorthand that instantly communicates the whole idea of speed. *Mario Andretti*. It's the fastest-sounding name in racing, and his signature roars by at 200 mph. While other drivers tend to be measured by their records—by wins and championships—Mario is more like a force you measure on the Richter scale.

He was born in northern Italy, and along with his family immigrated to the United States when he was 15. "I lived the American dream," he has said, "because I was able to pursue at a very early age what I set as my goals." In those early years—the 1960s—his goals called for

I could never beat Mario, but seeing how close I could get was a sort of benchmark.

winning every kind of race . . . sprint cars, stock cars, sports cars, and single-seaters . . . victories on the dangerous dirt tracks of Pennsylvania, on the high banks of Daytona, the wide, flat runways of Sebring, and the historic Speedway at Indianapolis. He was the gunslinger who rode into town and beat the best of the best, at their own game. He drove without a safety net, and you worried that he would take one risk too many. He liked to say that if everything seemed under control, he wasn't going fast enough. And while he didn't invent that phrase, Mario lived it as no one else has, before or since.

There is an invisible line that separates the merely great from that handful of champions who change the public's perception of their sport, redefining it in their own terms. Tiger Woods *is* golf . . . and Mario Andretti *is* racing. But how did this happen?

Winning the world championship was part of it. In 1978, Mario was driving a Lotus for Colin Chapman, and Chapman had designed Formula One's first ground-effect car, which revolutionized F1. Mario's grasp of speedway technology—of stagger and cross-weight—made the car nearly invincible, and in one year he won 6 of his 12 career grand prix.

He won races for Enzo Ferrari, too, including South Africa in 1971, the first he ever drove for the team. All told, Mario won 109 major races—but curiously, it is his defeats, especially at Indy, that have touched people's hearts. When he won the race in 1969, the victory was so decisive that it was taken for granted the 500 had found a new champion, and that many more wins would follow. But—as is well known—he never won Indy again, in 26 tries. Tom Carnegie saying "Andretti is slowing on the backstretch" has become part of Speedway culture. Even the most casual fans could share the heartbreak and wonder about the role of luck in racing, and in life. Mario has known the heights of success and the depths of failure, and has dealt graciously with both. "I am never bored," he once said.

Today, Mario is the family patriarch. His son Michael and grandson Marco have done immeasurable credit to the Andretti name. A Napa Valley winery bears his name, along with an extensive list of other entrepreneurial endeavors ranging from a Toyota dealership to car washes to video games.

He was voted "Driver of the Century" by the Associated Press, and the Italian government made him a *commendatore*, Italy's highest civilian honor, bestowed on only one other man from the world of racing, Enzo Ferrari.

His house is filled with trophies—shining, highly polished reminders of past glory. But he is very much a man of the moment. He can still cut a fast lap in an Indy car, and he's widely admired, his opinions sought out at the highest levels. He is our sport's finest ambassador.

"Who do you think you are—Mario Andretti?" There is only one person who can answer "yes" to that, and he has chosen to honor us with his presence here tonight . . .

Mario Andretti!

Monaco! The dullest race of the year, the most formulaic of the teases—but the most fun. You know you're going to start with a wide shot of the harbor, then zero in on the yachts. I like to include the big rock ("the giant immovable granite citadel"), but some years I go right to the cars. What comes next? Options include the royal family, black-and-white footage of the first race (1929), pretty girls on yachts, the casino, Senna's six wins, the menacing guardrails, and so on. Each year I wander among these jewels, searching for the fresh angle that I know is there, immured in the treasure vaults, waiting to be discovered.

Monaco '09

To anyone at sea, a harbor is a place of refuge and safety, and the harbor at Monaco, with its sturdy seawall and deep, azure water, is as protective and sheltering as any on the Mediterranean coast.

The welcoming harbor shelters the mariner; by contrast, the harsh demands of the track winding along its shore expose the F1 driver not only to the scrutiny of thousands of eyes staring down from balconies and grandstands, but also to the torment of his own self-doubt.

It is well known that great drivers absorb information in a way that makes time expand and the world slow down. Nowhere is that worth more than here—and nowhere does the driver who is less than the very best miss it more. To the masters of Monaco—Moss, Stewart, Senna—the narrow road looks a little wider; their minds stay clearer as they aim their cars at the jutting curbs, as they slice past the cold walls of steel, ambition and skill compressing their margin for error to a foot, and finally, to an inch.

At other tracks, a driver misjudges a turn and just runs wide. Not here. At other tracks, you need a stopwatch to tell how fast a driver is going; here in Monaco's confining canyons, you feel the speed, feel the genteel baroque elegance of the city shattered by the risks these men take.

In the harbor, the tides rise and fall in the comforting rhythms of the sea. On the track, it is life on the very edge, the drivers of Formula One at the limit, with nowhere to hide.

The Grand Prix of Monaco is . . . *next!*

Monaco '10

onaco is about seawater and champagne, about very rich people wearing very few clothes, about a giant immovable granite citadel and the fast, frail cars that race in its shadow.

Amid these contrasts, one fact stands out: Monaco, more than any other, is the grand prix drivers want most to win. Partly it's the history, stretching back to 1929; partly it's hanging with Al, Steffi, and the other castle folks; partly it's because the sponsors are all here. But mostly it's the momentum of an idea—that Monaco is the ultimate test of what counts the most in driving: nerve.

The corners are blind, the guardrails are right at the track's edge, there's a tunnel you take at 170, and a hairpin where 40 is too fast. There are no runoff areas worthy of the name. The streets are narrow, passing almost impossible. In fact, everything about this most famous of all F1 tracks is the exact opposite of what a modern circuit is supposed to be.

But . . . this is the place, more than any other, where the best get to show their stuff. Alain Prost, four wins; Michael Schumacher, five wins; and Ayrton Senna, with an incredible six wins . . . truly the man who broke the bank at Monte Carlo.

Pastel hotels, dented guardrails, chardonnay on the balcony, chaos and mayhem in the streets below . . . the Grand Prix of Monaco, the race that comes dressed in a tux—or a bikini—is . . . *next!*

Monaco '11

It isn't the floating pleasures of the sleek yachts.

It isn't the celebrities.

Or the prince.

Or the famed casino.

It's the walls.

The walls are the reality of Monaco to the modern F1 driver.

The guardrails pressing in against the edges of the narrow streets, the twisting course, a tunnel of steel.

The limits are unforgiving and absolute—no runoff areas here. Lesser men shrink from the walls, while each year an elite few brush so close to them as to transcend judgment and skill, entering a zone of utmost peril from which they draw utmost confidence. A dozen blind turns in two miles, drivers operating on instinct alone . . . 40 gearshifts in 75 seconds, the beating heart of the busiest lap in all of Formula One. The race through the streets—and between the walls—the Grand Prix of Monaco, the jewel of the Mediterranean, is . . . *next!*

Monaco '14

Monaco is a showcase for wealth—its harbor, jammed deck to teak deck with money that floats; its hotels, dressed up with necklaces of Ferraris and Lambos, money you can drive. And there's the casino, where the more money you lose, the richer you must be.

But once a year, starting in 1929, there's one week when wealth isn't measured by bank accounts or expensive toys. It's measured by the heartbeat between you and the guardrail, by the ambition that lets you see opportunity where others see only risk, by having luck when it counts most . . . those things are not for sale.

Nor can Monaco be imitated. The new tracks are vast expanses of asphalt with only painted stripes showing you where the course goes. In Monaco you know where to go because there's nowhere else to go. Left at Sainte-Dévote—forget it; there's a church in the way. Go straight at the hairpin, and you're in the lobby of the Fairmont hotel. Portier? No room for error here, as Ayrton Senna found out in 1988. Leading, he made a small mistake that would have gone unnoticed . . . everywhere but in Monaco. These are the same streets that were used in the black-and-white years, and the way everyday traffic gets around town today—when they're closed for racing, you walk.

The 71 Monaco Grand Prix have been run under the timeless gaze of this great granite rock. Conceived in the name of sport, its sense of place and its enduring history make this race the most coveted grand prix of all.

*I know the exact moment I discovered racing. I was 14, traveling
with my mother, and we were in the Edinburgh train station, about
to go to London. Looking around for a book for the trip, I bought one
with the strange title* Challenge Me the Race. *It turned out to be the
autobiography of Mike Hawthorn. He had just won the French GP at
Reims, and his name was splashed all over the papers. He went on to
win the Championship, only to die a couple of months later in a road
accident. Reims was the only race he won that year, and the victory was
bittersweet. His Ferrari teammate Luigi Musso was killed in the early
laps, and the great Juan Manuel Fangio retired at the end of the race.*

*I had wanted to write about this particular grand prix for some time,
and I was thrilled when Tom Bryant gave me the green light. It's rare
that an entire era has a kind of signature race, but Reims 1958 had
everything: the front-engine cars, the danger, the heroic driver (Fangio),
the camaraderie. I hope some of that comes through in this article.*

Height of an Era
ROAD & TRACK, JULY 2008

Fifty years ago, grand prix racing's postwar era was about to
end. Front-engine cars, amateur drivers, tracks that were
public roads—all would be gone within a very few years. But
nobody knew it then, and in the summer of 1958 a race was held that
was innocent of the future and that perfectly embodied the spirit of the
time. It was the French Grand Prix, run on July 6 outside Reims, a city
famous for its 13th-century cathedral—a Gothic masterpiece—and for
being the capital of France's Champagne region.

The central character of the story is Mike Hawthorn, who would win
the race in a 2.4-liter Ferrari Dino 246, leading from start to finish. He
was a tall, fair-haired 29-year-old Englishman who wandered around
the paddock wearing a tweed jacket and smoking a pipe. In the cockpit,
he sported a bow tie. His family owned and ran the Tourist Trophy

Garage; prize money was just gravy. Reims was his only win of the year, and it established him as Ferrari's team leader and a contender for the championship, in which he would defeat Stirling Moss by a single point. The race would also be remembered as the last GP for the great Juan Manuel Fangio, as well as the first for future World Champion Phil Hill. Ferrari's victory ended a two-year drought, but the celebration would be brief.

The track's layout dated back to 1925, when virtually every French track consisted of a long straight on a main road and two shorter straights on local roads, a rough triangle connecting three towns. The back straight at Reims was a two-mile blast down RN 31, the Reims-Soissons highway, and it sliced across golden wheat fields that stretched to the horizon. The course was 5.2 miles long and had two hairpins, three sweepers, and one terrifyingly fast right-hander just after the pits. Whenever Fangio went out to practice, the other drivers would gather there to watch. You'd hear him approaching, then he'd flash into sight as he came under one of the distinctive, tire-shaped Dunlop bridges. Just when you knew he had to back off, he would hurl the car into a four-wheel drift, scrubbing off exactly enough speed to get through without lifting. It was a maneuver most drivers would attempt once or twice a weekend; Fangio did it every time.

Hawthorn had beaten Fangio in a wheel-to-wheel battle at Reims five years ago, and he was one of a handful of drivers who, when the occasion demanded, could match him in the fast turn. ("Hairy flatters" was the way Hawthorn described taking it.) Mercurial—lazy and unfocused at times, coldly brilliant at others—Mike knew that when he was on, nobody was better, and he was on now. He'd gone out the moment practice began Wednesday evening, intent on winning the 100 bottles of Moët that went with being the first to lap at over 200 km/h. Two minutes, 23.9 seconds later, the champagne was his.

Meanwhile, his rival, Stirling Moss, was struggling, his English Vanwall overheating and down on power. Fifty years later, when I e-mailed him about the race, Stirling replied immediately, listing the revs he reached with each axle ratio he tried—just as if the race had been last week. Fangio was having a tough time, too, forced to sort out an all-new Maserati that had arrived a day late. He had started 50 GPs and won 24, a degree of superiority greater even than Michael Schumacher's. But this year he had only raced in the season-opener in Argentina, and paddock wisdom held that at age 47, he was about to hang it up.

Hawthorn was on the pole, with his teammate, 33-year-old Luigi Musso, beside him. Moss and Fangio were back in the third row. Mike liked his chances. With improvements to the Ferrari's suspension, he had finished second at Spa three weeks earlier, his best result in the season so far. He was just three points behind Moss, and it already seemed like one of them would win the championship that for the last four years had been Fangio's personal property.

Mike had accepted Stirling's offer of a ride out from Paris, but not before he'd made Stirling's wife, Katie, assure him that her husband had reformed and was now safe to ride with on public roads. They stopped for lunch in Soissons, where they met up with Harry Schell, a driver born in Paris of American parents living in France. The GP world was much smaller in 1958 than it is today, and slower-paced, because fewer races were held. Drivers often traveled together and stayed in the same hotels. No one had sponsors to look after, or entourages.

Although Stirling abstained from alcohol, most drivers considered drinking to be compulsory, and here Mike was in a class by himself. (He would have made short work of Kimi Raikkonen.) "Crumpet" was pursued with religious fervor at all times, day or night. Mike, in fact, had an illegitimate son living in Reims, the result of a one-night stand following his win over Fangio.

This year, the department of practical jokes was in high gear, with Harry Schell as the victim. Contemplating a romantic afternoon following lunch at their hotel, the Lion d'Or, Harry and his girlfriend returned to their room to find all the furniture missing. After a suitable interval the culprits, who included Moss, Musso, Phil Hill, and Dan Gurney, replaced it. But the look on Harry's face . . . didn't that call for an encore? That evening, they muscled Harry's Vespa sedan up to the second floor and parked it in front of the manager's office, complete with a vase of flowers on the roof and a For Sale sign. When the time came to take the car back downstairs, Fangio was game to drive it, but the course was judged too perilous even for him.

On race day, the sky was hazy with summer heat. The flags and banners hung limp. A 12-hour GT race begun at midnight had ended, but jazz-era dance music intended to liven it up still played over the PA, tinny and strangely unnerving. At two p.m., a 30-lap Formula 2 event began in which GP men Moss, Peter Collins, and Jean Behra competed. Moss and Behra dueled for the lead until Stirling's car lost oil pressure, leaving the Frenchman to win, with Collins in the lone Ferrari, second. Now it was almost time for the GP.

Engines were started, the throttles blipped for a minute or two, then shut down and the plugs changed. Of the 21 cars lined up in front of the pit boxes, 12 were Italian (Ferraris and Maseratis), most of them painted red, Italy's national racing color. The rest were the green of Great Britain (Vanwalls, BRMs, Lotuses, and the rear-engine Coopers of Jack Brabham and Roy Salvador). No advertising marred the lines of the cars, although automotive ads covered every square inch of the pit boxes and grandstands. Collins led Hawthorn around for a lap to point out where the asphalt was slick with oil dropped during the F2 race.

The major works entries took up the front half of the grid; in back of them, starting at the fifth row, was a ragtag collection of privately owned cars, including six aging Maseratis whose drivers would be having their own race within a race. The Maserati group included three Americans, each making his GP debut. Troy Ruttman had won Indy in 1952, and was curious about F1. He would finish 10th and never drive in another GP, his curiosity apparently satisfied. Carroll Shelby would retire from the race early but stick with F1 through seven others, and hook up with Aston Martin, with whom he would win Le Mans the next year.

Phil Hill, however, was totally committed to Formula One. He was already under contract with Ferrari to drive sports cars, and the step to F1 seemed natural. But Enzo kept telling him to wait, stringing him along with assurances that his time would come—and then not only not delivering but threatening to fire him if he so much as inquired about a ride with another team. Phil's epic, rain-soaked win at Le Mans in mid-June should have entitled him to at least a shot at F1; when he didn't get it, and Jo Bonnier offered to lend him his two-year-old Maserati for Reims, Phil's friends begged him to defy Enzo and race the Maser.

And, so far, it looked as if his gamble could pay off: With the exception of Francisco Godia-Sales, the Spanish millionaire who had Fangio qualify his car for him, Phil was the fastest of the independents, including Bonnier. Brabham was alongside him, his Cooper barely longer than the Maserati's hood. (Hill and Brabham were an interesting pair to be buried in the fifth row. Driving the little Cooper, Jack was destined to succeed Hawthorn as World Champion in 1959—and to win again the following year. Phil would become the 1961 champion, aboard a Ferrari.)

A cordon of French police cleared the grid. The engines were all running now, the sound magnified in the shallow canyon between the pit complex and the stands. All at once the roar jumped up an octave and the cars shot forward, emerging from beneath a cloud of blue tire smoke, then vanishing under the Dunlop Bridge.

Hawthorn was never a great starter, and he dropped to fourth as they streamed through the first turn. But his Ferrari was "going like a rocket," as he would put it in *Champion Year*, his book about the season, and he took the lead even before he reached the hairpin onto the back straight—a lead he would hold for the two hours, three minutes it would take to complete the 50-lap, 258-mile race. Behind him came a tight knot of cars, including three Vanwalls (Moss, Tony Brooks, and Stuart Lewis-Evans), Harry Schell's BRM, Fangio's Maserati, and the Ferraris of Collins and Musso. By the third lap, Musso broke free and set off after the leader.

From Musso's perspective, it was imperative that he come to grips with Hawthorn. He was the only top-line Italian driver left—Bonetto, Fagioli, Ascari, and Castellotti had all died at the wheel. Italy's honor rested with him now; he had the flag painted on his helmet. He got along with Hawthorn and Collins well enough, but it angered him that they were taking over the Ferrari team that by all rights should have been his. He'd ratted on Collins for wrecking that clutch at Le Mans and got him demoted to F2.

But Hawthorn had raised a fuss, and here was Collins, back in F1, with everything forgiven! The Brits had even agreed to split their prize money 50/50. They were such buddies, calling each other "mon ami mate" and saying things he couldn't understand. And Hill—obviously, this Maserati business was part of a scheme to break into F1.

As if racing wasn't trouble enough, Musso's deal to import Pontiacs from the States had somehow gone wrong. The night before the race, his partners in Rome had sent a threatening telegram, demanding cash. But Reims had by far the largest purse of the year: 10 million francs for the winner, enough to erase his debt.

By the ninth lap, about 22 minutes into the race, Hawthorn began lapping slower cars. He passed Ruttman and Shelby just after the pits. Fangio, close behind, saw Musso also go by the Americans and set up for the fast turn. Suddenly the Italian's car wobbled, then started to slide. At the same moment, Hawthorn, exiting the turn, checked his mirrors and caught a glimpse of the Ferrari sideways across the road. It went off backward, dropping out of sight in a ditch, and then Mike saw a big cloud of dust. The next time he came by, a helicopter was hovering above the scene, but it was gone the following lap. Musso had spun at Spa, too, mowing down a row of posts and caroming off a stone house. He'd been lucky then; Mike hoped he'd be lucky again.

Without Musso chasing him, Hawthorn felt the pressure ease. In practice he'd turned the V6 to 8,600 rpm, good for 180 mph in top gear. Now he was shifting at 8,400 and feathering the throttle on the straight. The Ferrari's drum brakes, usually inferior to the Vanwall's discs, felt solid. He was six-foot-two and accustomed to hunching down to keep out of the airstream, but Ferrari had built an additional two inches into this particular chassis, and Hawthorn for once could sit back in the cockpit. He hadn't won a GP in four years, but he knew the feeling of being on the way to a win, and he was having it now. His pit signals showed Fangio in second, 20 seconds back. *Déjà vu!* But on lap 24 the World Champion ducked into the pit, rejoining well back in seventh. Almost immediately, a furious battle for second erupted between Moss's Vanwall and Behra's BRM.

Moss had described the track as "boring" because of the long straights, but races here were often the most exciting of the year to watch. Thanks to the drafting, which the English called *slipstreaming*, cars circulated in tight packs, NASCAR-style. Moss and Behra took up where they had left off in the F2 race, and for nearly 40 minutes they thrilled the crowd by exchanging positions several times a lap. The duel ended when the BRM's fuel pump failed on lap 39. By then both other Vanwalls were out, and Stirling's was falling apart. All he could do was nurse it to the finish. At least he was safe from attack from behind: the third-place car, the Ferrari of Count Wolfgang von Trips, was more than a minute behind.

Meanwhile, Hawthorn was about to lap Fangio; but instead of going by, he backed off to allow him to finish on the lead lap—a spontaneous gesture that showed Mike's respect for the maestro. Six laps to go, and his pit signals hadn't indicated anything about fastest lap, so he dropped back before the long straight, hit 8,700, and then brought the Ferrari smoothly home to the checker. Moss arrived 24 seconds later.

Collins, it turned out, had sacrificed a critical lap of gas to lead Haw-thorn around before the start; he was pushing his car to the line when Fangio passed him for fourth. Jack Brabham was sixth, foreshadowing the imminent success of rear-engine cars. A euphoric Phil Hill was seventh, first of the old Maseratis.

Ferrari had won its first race since midsummer of 1956, and Hawthorn was tied with Moss for the championship lead. Reason to celebrate, but Mike found the mood in the pits restrained: Musso's injuries were serious. At the hospital, Mike and Peter encountered a friend of Luigi's who told them he had just died. The dust Mike had seen was the Ferrari digging into soft earth; it had flipped end over end, thrown Musso out, and crushed him when it landed.

All four of Ferrari's drivers that July day were star-crossed, and the remaining three would also soon be dead—Collins in a month, Hawthorn in January of the next year, von Trips in 1961. Collins and von Trips would die racing; Mike would win the championship, announce his retirement, get engaged, and then be killed in a high-speed road accident.

Four more of the 21 drivers who started the GP that day would die racing. To us now, the level of risk they accepted seems appalling. But their frame of reference was World War II, with its ethos of sacrifice, of lives that were short but lived to the fullest. Danger was the currency of their sport. Drivers respected one another, and fans venerated them, merely for their willingness to get in the car. They didn't disdain safety; they just never thought about it. Phil Hill, a reasonable man, drove at Reims in a short-sleeved shirt, wearing a helmet made from material about as thick as a piece of heavy cardboard.

Today, we know how rapidly the sport was to develop, the huge industry it would become, and it makes Hawthorn and company look a little quaint, like Don Quixotes rushing around in funny old cars. The trick is to forget about today and remember that 50 years ago, our modern world didn't exist—and that the slash of red moving quickly through golden wheat fields under a hazy blue French sky was the apotheosis of an era.

The discovery of aerodynamic downforce, the exponential increase in horsepower, tires getting wider and wider—the late 1960s saw speeds increase so much as to bring about a fundamental change in the sport. I was there, in the thick of it, and this article is shamelessly autobiographical.

Racing's Golden Age of Speed

ROAD & TRACK, AUGUST 2002

Until the last few years, it was understood that each new crop of racing cars would be faster than the last, that new lap records would be set, and that racing was part of a culture of technology that was leading to a better world. Every now and then, a specific innovation such as disc brakes or rear-engine cars would cause a jump in the graph.

In September 1966, the graph was about to jump again, but this time three major developments—in tires, horsepower, and aerodynamics—would hit the sport at the same time, creating a giant spike, a surge of speed and exuberance that would last until the 1972 Indy 500—five years and eight months that would utterly transform the world of racing. I was along for the ride, driving in everything from Le Mans to the Baja 1000 to Indy, and I was there in Saint-Jovite, Canada, on September 11, 1966, the first day of practice for the all-new Can-Am series . . . and the day the golden age of speed began.

The sky was so blue it was hard on the eyes. The cars were unknown quantities, hybrid hot rods with American V8s bolted into European chassis—an explosive combination that owed its existence to rules that were conspicuous by their absence (you could really build anything as long as the wheels were sort of enclosed).

In the months leading up to the Can-Am, the engines had gone from small-block Olds and Fords to big-block Chevys, a jump of more than 100 horsepower. This had produced excessive wheelspin, which led to tires that were wider and had less tread. By Saint-Jovite they were almost slick, and as wide as they were tall. Wheelspin had been reduced, but what the new, grippy tires had really done was to increase cornering speed. Brian Redman, doing a back-to-back test of the old tires and the new ones, reported an improvement of five seconds.

Overnight, Can-Am cars replaced Formula One cars as the fastest road-racing cars ever, so visibly faster than anything we had ever seen that you could sense something not necessarily good was about to happen.

It didn't take long. As practice began, I was out in my new McLaren getting the feel of things when the Australian Paul Hawkins came by in his Lola. A lap later, as he headed toward a rise that comes early in the straight, the Lola's nose lifted, and the car—already going the speed cars used to reach at the end of the straight—was transformed into a wing, soaring up and over, landing upside down, then spinning along the track.

A few minutes later when we had Hawkins safely out of what was left of the car, we looked back at the hill crest where he had taken off, and it seemed impossibly far away. The next day, Hugh Dibley lost control at the same place, flying so high that his car seemed to flutter to the ground like a falling leaf. We were looking at a new phenomenon—flying cars—and a new set of dimensions.

By race day every available scrap of aluminum had been turned into hastily improvised spoilers. I thought the added drag meant we were sacrificing speed for safety, but then we noticed that the bigger the spoiler, the better the lap time . . .

Exactly a week later, it all began to make sense. Jim Hall's Chaparrals had missed Saint-Jovite, but when the matched pair of white 2Es rolled into the paddock at Bridgehampton sporting huge airfoils, as wide as the car and mounted at eye level above the rear deck, the message was clear: Air, which just a week before had caused two cars to fly, would now be used to drive cars down onto the road. There amid the sand dunes of Eastern Long Island, you could see the future. A whole new way to make cars fast had arrived, right on the heels of the big horsepower and the wide tires. And there was more to come, this time from the world of Formula One.

Just nine months after Bridgehampton, again among sand dunes, another revolutionary car was introduced. In Zandvoort, Holland, at the Dutch GP, Colin Chapman unveiled the Lotus 49. Until the 49, engines were developed independent of the chassis. Chapman hacked off the chassis just behind the driver and used the engine as a stressed member to which the rear suspension was attached, thus pioneering the concept of engine configuration as part of the overall design of the car. While this was important, it was the 49's engine that triggered a revolution.

In 1966, rules had doubled the allowable displacement of an F1 engine from 1.5 liters to 3.0; commissioned by Ford, Cosworth built an engine for the new formula. Designated the DFV, the compact V8 was mated to a Hewland gearbox, and the combination provided teams with an "off the shelf" drivetrain that could win. It was as if F1 had suddenly been deregulated. Second-tier teams became competitive, and new teams sprang into existence. Grids overflowed with cars. The races were close.

More makes and drivers won. The "kit-car" era, as it was pejoratively known, freed designers to concentrate on the chassis, and they turned out cars that were increasingly light, nimble . . . and fast. One race, the Italian GP of 1971, tells the story. Twenty-two cars started and five (each a different make) finished in a virtual dead heat. Winner Peter Gethin averaged more than 150 mph, the fastest grand prix in history, and a record that still stands.

Just one year after the debut of the Lotus 49, Chapman introduced commercial sponsorship to Formula One. This new money came from tobacco companies and others that were outside the traditional circle of automotive sponsors and, like the DFV, it increased the number of players in F1. Their influence would soon be felt on an issue that was at the very core of the sport: danger.

Throughout the 1950s and well into the '60s, the people in racing were of a generation who had either been in, or remembered, World War II. No one would have admitted it, but the danger was condoned—even welcomed—because it allowed men to achieve in peacetime the sort of heroic stature usually reserved for combat heroes. But then came the spring of 1968. Four F1 drivers—Jim Clark, Mike Spence, Ludovico Scarfiotti, and Jo Schlesser—were killed, and while only Schlesser died in an F1 car, the deaths stunned the F1 fraternity. Worse yet, speeds were about to jump again.

Surprisingly, it took F1 designers a while to catch on to what was going on in the Can-Am and in endurance racing, where the winged Chaparral 2F had won at Brands Hatch in 1967. It wasn't until the spring of 1968 that the benefits of downforce were first applied in Formula One. For Monaco, Colin Chapman (again) fitted a Lotus 49 with stubby dive planes at the front and an upswept spoiler at the back. (Graham Hill drove; it won.) Two weeks later, at Spa, Ferrari designer Mauro Forghieri mounted an anemic airfoil above the engine—F1's first wing.

By the British GP in late July, however, wings were in full flight. Chapman was running a large rear foil on tall struts about the diameter of a toothpick. And the cars were incredibly fast: In just two years, lap times at Brands Hatch dropped by more than seven seconds! By the spring of 1969, F1 cars had wings front and back, and they were blasting around like fighter planes.

Once again, you could sense trouble, and it came at Montjuich Park, in Barcelona, Spain. The wings on both works Lotuses collapsed at the same, very fast, part of the circuit, and only by blind luck did Hill and Jochen Rindt survive. To the surprise of many, suspension-mounted wings were promptly banned.

Just a few years before, driving the winged cars would have been in the line of duty. But now a new generation had arrived on the scene, along with a practical Scotsman named John Young Stewart. Jackie had a life-threatening crash at Spa in 1966, where he was trapped, soaked with gas in his BRM, and he was ready to speak out against unnecessary risks.

His track record had shown him to be a man of unquestioned courage, which brought grudging respect to his campaign for guardrails and other safety measures. He was able to build a constituency among the people who were part of the expansion brought about by the new teams and the widening circle of sponsors.

To these people, many of them young, the best part of racing was the excitement and the money; getting killed seemed pointless. If sponsors invested in a driver, they needed to have him stick around. If a family with young kids came to the races, you didn't want them to see drivers killed. So Jackie got his guardrails, and, as drivers like Bruce McLaren, John Surtees, Jack Brabham, and Dan Gurney began building cars, no one had to tell them that the wheels should stay on.

As the shadow of death receded, the world of racing began to expand. Here in the United States, Formula 5000 became a stock-block version of F1. The Trans-Am was a showcase for Detroit's hot-selling pony cars. As the core grew, the fringe grew with it. The romance of the dusty run down the Baja Peninsula from Ensenada to La Paz led to the birth of off-road racing as an organized sport.

In the Cannonball Baker Sea-to-Shining-Sea Memorial Trophy Dash (immortalized in the movie *Cannonball Run*), the idea was to dodge the cops in a sprint from the Red Ball Garage in New York to the pier in Redondo Beach, California. If you had a hot thumb, you could show up at your local slot-car parlor with a Cox Chaparral complete with a wing, sponge tires, and a rewound motor.

World events kept pace. In 1967, Dr. Christiaan Barnard transplanted a human heart. In 1968, director Stanley Kubrick gave us *2001: A Space Odyssey*—and a year later, there was Neil Armstrong walking on the moon. But perhaps the best symbol of the times was a breakfast cereal, Kaboom, that featured marshmallow stars and a sugar content of 43 percent. You needed the sugar just to keep up.

At least I did. I remember my first Baja 1000, driving a Peccary (which meant "pig," which it was) and breaking down in the middle of nowhere. I hitched a ride on a stake truck loaded with tortoises, then chartered a flight to Las Vegas so I wouldn't miss practice for the Can-Am. I walked into the Stardust Hotel at midnight still wearing my driving suit, opened my wallet, and sand poured out all over the desk. From Las Vegas, I went on to a race in Japan, where motorsport was the new national frenzy. A week after that, I was home racing slot cars with my brothers on the 80-foot, four-lane track that my mother had had built by professional carpenters right in her front hall.

In the midst of this golden age of speed, it was ironic that the two great races of the world—Indy and Le Mans—were left behind and had to catch up. Le Mans had seemed to peak in 1967 when Gurney and A. J. Foyt won in Ford's awesome 7.0-liter Mk IV, covering over 3,251 miles in 24 hours and running 213 mph down the Mulsanne straight. The fastest lap was 147 mph, and that, for the moment, was enough speed for the organizers.

In 1968 a chicane was installed just before the pits, and the regulations barred the big-engine prototypes; the fastest lap dropped to 138 mph. But the next year, the rules were relaxed to permit manufacturers to enter a new 5.0-liter Sports class, provided they were willing to produce 25 identical cars. Porsche (gunning for its first overall win) and Ferrari built cars that were pure prototypes—Can-Am cars with roofs, mass produced. The next two years were to be the fastest in the history of the track.

I was in both races, driving for Ferrari against the Porsche on-slaught. Imagine rushing down the Mulsanne straight in the early laps, 20 Porsches and Ferraris clumped together, drafting at 230 mph, the turbulence so bad that you had to steer vigorously just to keep the thing going straight—or what you hoped was straight, because most of the time the view was blocked by the rear wing of the car ahead, and you had cars on either side, which kept you from glancing down at the edges of the road.

The Ferraris had heavy steering that would get unnervingly light when I was close behind another car, causing memories of Hawkins and Dibley to flash through my mind. And it was the same for the Porsches, especially the ones with the very long tails. I remember Pedro Rodríguez off to my left in a 917, white as a sheet and steering like mad, but the car wasn't responding, and I wondered if his front wheels were doing much more than just brushing the road.

In 1971, the lap record was jacked up to 155 mph, and the total distance run—3,315 miles—eclipsed even the Gurney/Foyt record that was set before the installation of the chicane. Was this too fast? The organizers thought so. They changed the rules again, relegating our Ferraris and Porsches to museums, and then they slowed the track. Never again would so many cars travel so fast for so long on public roads. In France, or anywhere else.

As racing roared into the 1970s, the one track that appeared to have everything was Indianapolis. Basking in the Memorial Day sun, the Speedway was the home of racing's oldest and grandest traditions, the biggest crowds, and the richest purse, and when you heard track announcer Tom Carnegie bellowing, "It's a new track record!," you knew, thrillingly, that the sport itself had just been redefined.

Except that, in 1970, Indianapolis was a technological backwater. The innovative turbine-powered cars that threatened the establishment in 1967 and '68 had been eliminated by a rule change, leaving a field of cars that were superbly crafted but conceptually dated. Downforce was minimal because the big idea at Indy was still to design for the straights, not the corners. The pole speed had edged upward from 161 mph in 1965 to 170 mph—just 9 mph in six years.

Enter McLaren. For 1971, their designer Gordon Coppuck drew an Indy car, designated the M16, which borrowed heavily from the Lotus 72, a radical, wedge-shaped F1 car with the radiators mounted on the sides rather than in the nose. McLaren sold an M16 to Roger Penske, and Mark Donohue developed it, along with engineer Don Cox. At the Speedway, the dark blue Sunoco Special ran 178 mph right off the trailer.

I remember arriving the next day and finding everyone, including Mark, in a state of shock. In the days leading up to qualifying, the team would polish the car all day, then roll it out at five p.m. when the track was cooling down. The next thing you would hear was Tom Carnegie announcing a new lap record and the crowd roaring. Then the car, still gleaming, would be towed back into the garage. Mark would not even have broken a sweat.

In qualifying, Donohue was conservative on his setup, and Peter Revson, in a team McLaren, went 178.696 mph to edge him for the pole. In one year speeds had shot up almost as much as they had in the previous six. Indy was now part of racing's golden age of speed, an age that would reach its climax—and its end—at the Speedway the very next year.

Indy, 1972. Bobby Unser's turbocharged Eagle, an elegant derivative of the M16, took the pole at the staggering speed of 195.941 mph. This was a jump of more than 17 mph, the biggest increase, ever, in Indy history. And Bobby wasn't the only one to go fast. Incredibly, even the slowest car in the field was quicker than Revson's pole time of the year before. The M16 had shown that Indy was more about corners than straights, and the new cars had capitalized on that. But the horsepower boys, feeling left out, had cooked up some new turbo systems for the venerable Offenhauser, and the word was that Bobby qualified with over 1,200 horsepower. (I qualified seventh at a positively sedate 184.379 mph, but even at that speed, acceleration off the turns—at over 175 mph—was so brutal I was pinned against the seat.)

As in the first days of the Can-Am almost six years before, this great blast of unbridled speed came because of simultaneous advances in tires, horsepower, and downforce. In the almost 30 years since then, nothing like that has happened again in racing. Dramatic and exciting innovations (such as ground effects and electronics) have occurred, but they have arrived politely, one at a time, and they have been contained, at least somewhat, by the rules.

The golden age was the expression of a spirit of extravagance that burst onto the scene without warning, condensing decades of progress into less than six years. I miss it.

Calling him "Jim" would have been out of the question, and Mr. Hall went too far the other way. He was either reclusive or shy, or maybe both—a mysterious figure who rarely stopped to chat between his car and the motor home.

Introduction for Road Racing Drivers Club Honoree: Jim Hall

LONG BEACH, CALIFORNIA, APRIL 12, 2012

He was tall and thin, a man of few words. With his cowboy hat pulled down, shading his eyes, he could have been a gunslinger out of the Old West. There was an air of mystery about him; you wondered: Exactly who was Jim Hall? For a man whose successes had thrust him into the spotlight, surprisingly little was known. He was an enigma, a moving target.

First he was the teenager rich enough to buy and race Ferraris and Maseratis as if they were toys. Then he was the F1 driver, far from home, holding his own against the best in the world.

Next, he was the reclusive innovator, the engineer building cars called Chaparrals in Midland, Texas, a place remote from the racing world but totally self-sufficient, complete with its own track, rattlesnake raceway, and a secret pipeline running straight from Midland to GM's R & D skunk works.

At the track, Hall was not one to pal around; in interviews he made a point of saying as little as possible. Some thought he was shy, others, that he was aloof. To me, he was a man with a lot on his mind, and he wasn't about to take the time to tell anyone what that was.

It was very much in character that many of his designs focused on something invisible: air. Drawing on his experience building model airplanes, Jim understood air as a palpable substance, its movement over a car to be exploited in an endless variety of ways. His first cars, like the 1965 Sebring winner, were strikingly compact, designed to keep air from working against them, a theme he would return to with the extreme streamlining of the 2H. His 1966 2E is possibly the most exciting car ever built, with rear-mounted radiators, a semiautomatic gearbox, and its signature giant airfoil, which converted air into downforce to improve cornering. It was driven by Hall and America's World Champion, Phil Hill. The 2E's refined successor, the 2F, was also driven by Hill, and it won the Manufacturers Championship race at Brands Hatch in 1967.

But just as we began to think of Jim as a designer first and a driver second, a terrifying crash in Las Vegas very nearly killed him; he was burned and broke both his legs. The loyalty he inspired in his men showed when longtime members of his team, such as Franz Weiss and Troy Rogers, showed up at the hospital day after day—not because Jim was their boss, but because he was their friend.

His most radical car was just two years down the road: the Chaparral 2J, also known as the box it came in. A snowmobile engine powered fans that sucked the air from under the car, creating a zone of negative pressure that glued it to the track.

The 2J brought to an end a decade of innovation that changed forever the way racing cars would be designed, and many thought it would be Jim's last hurrah. In fact, there was much more to come: a second decade at the forefront of American racing, this time as Jim Hall, car owner. In the mid-1970s his team—with Brian Redman driving—won three consecutive F5000 championships with a Chaparral-prepared Lola.

Then Jim went after the big one, the Indy 500, winning 1978 with Al Unser Sr., and two years later with Johnny Rutherford, who drove the bright yellow Pennzoil Chaparral, a ground-effect car that was conceptually a direct descendant of the air-sucking 2J. Jim Hall is the most innovative designer in the history of American racing, and he was a top driver, a combination that puts him in a class by himself. But what has impressed me the most through the years has been his boundless curiosity, his quest to understand the fundamentals of how things work. Along the way, the mysterious side of Jim Hall has begun to fade, the shadows lift. Today there's even a Chaparral museum in Midland, displaying the cars that are his legacy, and whose secrets were there all along, hiding in plain sight, as car by car he taught us new ways to see.

We honor a very special person tonight—or, rather, he honors us with his presence here . . .

Mr. Jim Hall.

This article is particularly significant to me because it is the story of my last race. At the end there's a description of the convivial atmosphere at a restaurant (Siebkens). As the party reached a sort of crescendo of hilarity and camaraderie, I thought at the time that all good things must eventually come to an end, and of course, you want them to end well, if possible.

Here I was with plenty of vodka, Brian Redman was doing the Spoon Trick (where a spoon hangs from the end of one's nose, defying gravity), David Hobbs was fortifying himself for—what? We'd soon find out . . .

Stopping now would mean finishing on a high note. I had just driven a beautiful car into second place in a major race, on a historic track (Road America). With our finish, Brian had clinched the IMSA championship—would things ever be any better?

So I retired, right then. I didn't tell anyone, because I wasn't sure it would still seem like a good idea the next morning. Author Tom McGuane wrote that the night sometimes writes a check the morning can't cash, and I didn't want to have to un-retire.

Fast Company

ROAD & TRACK, MARCH 1982

The offer to drive the Ralph Kent Cooke / Roy Woods–owned Lola T600 came as a total surprise. For most of the season I had been appearing at race tracks in the company of TV crews, not racing teams, and I thought people imagined I had retired. But here was Brian Redman, Cooke-Woods' driver and the leader in the Camel GT championship, inviting me to drive for the team at Elkhart Lake.

I accepted with mixed feelings. It had been two months since my last race, and much longer than that since I had driven a pure racing machine with the Lola's 600-plus horsepower. Brian is a good friend, and it was obvious that Cooke-Woods had invested plenty in this effort; I would feel terrible if my rustiness spoiled their chances.

The race was three weeks away, but there was little I could do to prepare. I had spent years driving Can-Am and Formula 5000 cars, which
had similar performance to the Lola, and I knew that when driving these
big cars you cross a threshold into a world that does not allow for a single
moment of lapsed concentration. The speed is so great everywhere on
the track that controlling the car calls for a nonstop flow of reactions
and decisions. This is something you cannot practice in a slower car.

Nevertheless I went to Mosport a week before Elkhart Lake and
tuned up as best I could with 20 laps in a Mazda. I also introduced
myself to the Cooke-Woods crew, and was invited to try the cockpit of
the Lola to see if I would fit. Then I watched as Brian, co-driving with
Eppie Wietzes, finished second behind the Andial Porsche 935 of Rolf
Stommelen and Harald Grohs. This was the first time the Lola had
finished behind a Porsche.

"In theory," Brian told me, "the Lola should be faster in the turns,
especially the high-speed ones where the ground effects and the overall
aerodynamics work best. But because the Porsche has a huge power
advantage—fully 200 bhp if it's one with the latest modifications and
the boost is turned up all the way—they can afford to run their wings
at very steep angles, and they wind up with almost as much downforce
as we have."

Mosport had brought Brian a giant step closer toward clinching the
championship. If Bobby Rahal, his only pursuer, scored no points at
Elkhart Lake, and Brian and I finished third or better, that would wrap it
up. Mosport had been a six-hour race, while Elkhart Lake, a 500-miler,
would be shorter and, because of the smooth track, easier.

The team appeared confident that reliability would not be a problem. And why not? This car, in the six races it had run, *had yet to break
down.* John David Bright, the team's chief mechanic, had been with
the car from the moment construction had started in England, and he
told me, "Sam, the hubs, the halfshafts, all the components you might
worry about are just fantastic. We check them, of course, but then they
go right back on."

Ironically, the team's closest call had occurred in the opening laps of Laguna Seca, the very first race for the Lola.

"I got myself so wound up over the car's debut," Brian told me, "that the night before the race I got about three hours' sleep. Then right off, right from the green flag, the handling felt wrong, as if the rear end was steering itself somehow. Well, you know Laguna—a crash there would have written off the car. But somehow I just couldn't bring myself to pit. Then things started to get *better*, which made no sense at all, and in the end we managed to win.

"What had happened was, we started with a loose wheel nut on the right rear. The wheel battered so hard against the nut that the nut actually broke the circlip on the end of the shaft, and at that point we were maybe a half-inch of thread away from disaster. But then by luck the wheel took a proper set against the nut, and the way Eric Broadley designed it, the spinning of the wheel will actually *tighten* the nut back on. I kept that nut as a souvenir, incidentally."

I watched John Bright load the car after Mosport, and for a moment before it disappeared into the transporter, its long envelope body was silhouetted against the sky. In five days I would be at the wheel.

Friday
Practice: 1:00–1:45 p.m.
Practice: 4:30–5:00 p.m.

Friday at Elkhart Lake was warm and clear. When I arrived mid-morning the team's transporter was already positioned, along with a rented motor home, in the least-crowded corner of the Road America paddock. The Lola was being polished. Brian took it out first.

A lap at Road America is four miles around, and to those waiting in the pits the car is out of sight for nearly two minutes. It comes into view taking the last turn, and you see it accelerating up the hill toward the pits. Then it flashes by and disappears into a dark tunnel of trees. The Porsches come past with a hard, concussive blast, seeming to shoulder the air aside, while the Lola slips by almost unnoticed.

Very little practice time was scheduled for the weekend, and Brian was determined that I drive a few laps in each session. Both of us would be under pressure: Brian, to set up the car in a minimum amount of time, and me, to learn all I could in what was obviously a cram course.

Accordingly, when Brian pitted and I took the wheel, no ceremony was made of my impending first drive. In a moment I was buckled in and heading up pit lane.

At the first turn I noticed that the car cornered with no body roll whatsoever. Exiting the second turn, the Lola's yellow fenders were outlined against a field as lush as a lawn. A spectator bridge loomed up and was gone, and as the speed rose the woods began to press in from both sides. The car's acceleration was as violent in third as it had been in second.

Road America is billiard-table smooth, the roadbed and pavement the pride of its creator, Cliff Tufte, formerly a highway contractor. On this perfect surface the stiffly sprung Lola felt as if it were waiting to do something sudden and unexpected. This was particularly true in the slower corners, which Tufte put in to simulate intersections. In lesser cars there is a monotony to these turns—Peter Revson used to call them Mickey Mouse—but the Lola's tautness coupled with its hair-trigger acceleration transformed them into corners requiring the utmost in balance and timing. By contrast, in the long sweeping carousel and the ultra-fast swerve just after it, the car's ground-effect system gave the car far more adhesion than I was prepared, so far, to use.

Meanwhile, I discovered I was too big for the cockpit. My head was banging into the roof, and each time I needed to move my foot from the accelerator to the brake I had to push myself up in the seat so my knee could clear the underside of the dash. I had been afraid this might happen because the car was set up perfectly for Brian, who is two inches shorter than I am, and in a cockpit where every dimension is critical, the bigger man usually has problems.

I had made three laps when the session ended. Back in the paddock, Brian and I had a look at the seat. A provision existed for moving it back, but it could not be done quickly, in a pit stop. I did not like the idea of compromising Brian's seating position, as he would be doing the lion's share of the driving, so I said I would give it another try the way it was.

As the second session began, most of the cars started turning representative times. The Porsches of John Fitzpatrick, Gianpiero Moretti, John Paul Jr. and Sr., and Rolf Stommelen were faster than our Lola. This had been the pattern of the season: The top Porsches would be faster in practice and qualifying when they ran with their boost up. Brian, despite his amazing record of four wins and two seconds, had yet to start a race from the pole.

When I went out in the car again it was remarkable how many of the details of driving, such as reading the instruments and shifting, were already becoming second nature. The seating position, however, was as cramped as before.

Saturday
Qualifying: 9:15–9:45 a.m.
This was my last chance to drive the car before the race, and it hinged upon Brian being able to cut a good qualifying lap and still have time to turn the car over to me. I watched anxiously from the pits, hoping he would get a break in the traffic. When it came, on his sixth lap, Brian made the most of the opportunity, qualifying the Lola in fourth place. The next lap he was in the pits, and time remained for me to do three laps before the end of the session.

It was exactly what I needed. I cut my first halfway decent lap. Also, I realized without question I had to get the seat moved back.

Brian willingly agreed to move the seat, even though it meant he would have to stretch for the pedals. Then we spent 20 minutes practicing our driver change, the Lola alone at one end of the long pit lane. Next, the car was pushed to the paddock and the crew erected a nylon canopy that extended fully 25 feet from the truck. The body and wheels were removed from the car and the chassis placed on jack stands. In the shadowless and diffused light, individual parts and pieces of the car, no longer subordinate to the whole, assumed distinctive personalities of their own.

The afternoon stretched ahead. No engine change was planned, thanks to the proven reliability of the team's Gerald Davis–built Chaparral engines. These were 350-cubic-inch Chevrolets with beefed-up NASCAR blocks and GM aluminum heads, and they had never failed in either a race or a practice.

Watching the crew carefully checking the car, it was hard to believe that, with the exception of John, the men had only been with the team for a few weeks. In mid-June, Ralph Cooke and Roy Woods decided to split with Garretson Enterprises, which had initially prepared the car, and Brian had been asked to form a new team.

Mike Brown, formerly with Ensign in Formula One and Condor Racing (another Cooke operation), was hired along with Mike Moyta, a skilled fabricator and truck driver. Steve Edwards, an apprentice at Lola, was vacationing in the United States, and Brian persuaded Eric Broadley to "loan" Steve for a month. But that was it: just four men.

Brian's influence had been felt from the very beginning of the whole T600 project, Cooke-Woods and Lola importer Carl Haas having made an extremely timely and astute decision to involve him in every phase of the car's construction and development.

Brian, you see, was spoiling for a comeback. Since his near-fatal Can-Am crash in 1977, he had established that he was once again a winner, but he had yet to steamroller his way through a season the way he had in the past. Think back to 1973, when he had scored five wins in F5000, and to 1974, when he had won three and took the championship. Then in 1975 it was four wins and a second championship, beating Mario Andretti. In 1976, a third championship and three more wins. Meanwhile, he was adding regularly to his list of long-distance racing victories, running up the total to more than 40, and establishing himself as the world's number-one endurance driver.

When you win that often it is partly because you need to win very badly, and partly because of what can only be described as special insight.

There are very few really fast drivers around to begin with, and the long-term difference between them is never a question of pure speed. The difference is that the great driver will grasp the essence of what it will take to win, while another driver does not. As a result, the great driver usually makes things seem effortless. Brian is this way.

A non-working visitor to the team during the weekend was Max Sardou, the French engineer who had been hired in the car's design stages for his experience with skirtless ground-effect cars. Max told me that the interaction between the underside of the T600 and the ground creates three times the downforce that the car would have if, hypothetically, it was moving along through the air like a plane. He explained that the air actually *swirls* through the Venturi tunnels, and he claimed that his design created 95 percent as much downforce as would have been possible in a skirted car. He also told me that the Lola's downforce increases as the car slides—the reverse of what occurs with skirted cars.

Throughout the afternoon, the chassis could be seen with various pairs of legs sticking out from under it. Sometimes they belonged to Max and me, sometimes to Max and Brian. At one point Max, Brian, John, and Carl Haas were all under the car at once, transforming the Lola into a giant spider!

Sunday
Warm-up: 10:00–10:30 a.m.
Race: 12:00 noon (125 laps, 500 miles)

We were directly behind the Andial Porsche on the grid. Brian nodded toward Stommelen and Grohs and said to me, "Based on their form as of this moment, that's the best pairing of drivers in this race." To their right, on the pole, was the bright blue Porsche of the John Pauls, father and son. They had won this race last year. Beside us was the Budweiser Lola of Chris Lord and Jim Adam, while a row behind was John Fitzpatrick, the defending IMSA champion.

"Welcome back to big-time auto racing," Brian said to me, laughing.

But the remark stuck: I realized that without admitting it to myself, I had wondered, now and then, if I would ever again be in the thick of a major race. The trouble was, Brian had put the car where it was in the grid, not me. In my mind I was still several seconds a lap from really being "back."

I walked through the rows of cars to our pit. It was another perfect day, cloudless and warm. On an impulse I crossed through the paddock and watched the start from the spectator area near the third turn. Brian lost time early on, thanks to the Porsches twisting up their boost for a couple of laps, but then he started to hold them. It all looked so easy, seen from the hillside among people eating lunches from picnic hampers.

I walked back to the pits, put my helmet on, and waited. At first, Brian had run third behind Stommelen and John Paul Jr., but he passed Paul for second, and when Stommelen pitted for fuel, the Lola was out front for two laps.

Our stop took a few seconds longer than it should have: For a terrible moment, I could not fit my arm through the left loop of the shoulder harness. As I accelerated up the pit lane, I was in second place behind the Pauls, but the moment I entered the track, I knew things were going to be tough, because Moretti's red 935 was no more than 20 yards back.

I knew it was foolhardy to fight the duel with Moretti, but I left my braking to the last instant anyway, and was startled when the Lola fishtailed sharply. I missed the apex and that was it; Moretti was past. The instability under braking meant too much rear-brake bias. I started to use the bias adjuster, but then I realized Brian would have made the correction himself unless there was some reason not to. (There was; worried after practice that the wear rate was too high on the front pads, Brian had biased the rears more heavily for the race, but had forgotten to tell me!)

Now Stommelen loomed up. I was having trouble with all the slow turns, either sliding wildly or not getting the throttle open soon enough. Was the throttle sticking? I could not be sure. Much more of this and I was going off the road; I let the Porsche through.

I was hot and cramped, but there was no time to think about it. Beyond the car's blunt nose, endless bunches of slower cars would clog the track for several laps, then suddenly I would burst into the clear, and a smooth ribbon of road would stretch ahead. Brian has his pit signals indicate how far he is behind the leader (never mind how many cars are in between), and I knew I was dropping back faster than Brian could hope to recover.

After the pit stop, I went to the motor home and found it deserted, the air conditioner purring. I lay down and thought hard about the track. By then I had taken each of the turns pretty well at one point or another, so I tried to construct a "perfect" lap in my mind. A few minutes before I was due to drive again, I discarded my sweat-sodden fireproof underwear and realized that I felt much less bulky without it.

Back at the wheel, I exited the pits onto a clear track. Suddenly I felt right, my uncertainties gone. In my first stint I had lost roughly a minute and a half to the leaders; Brian in his second stint had neither gained nor lost ground. Now on a good lap I, too, was able to hold us even. With the front pads worn down, the brake bias was perfect, although I had to push the pedal farther before the brakes would respond. Without the underwear I fitted the seat at last. Moretti had broken down, and we were running third, which would give Brian the championship.

In the long, fast carousel turn I pushed harder and harder each lap, amazed that I was still below the car's potential. In slow turns the Lola cornered as well as other cars I have driven, but in the fast stuff its capabilities exceeded anything I had ever experienced. The enormous downforce generated by the ground effect literally compressed the sidewalls of the front tires, making steering a physical battle. Huge g-forces wrenched at my head and neck. Forget the delicate balancing act that used to go with Fangio's drifts; the faster the turn, the more the Lola stuck to the road.

Then my stint was over and Brian was once again at the wheel. An hour remained. I stood behind the pits, relieved not to have made any mistakes, disappointed not to have been faster. The Pauls' Porsche came through the pits, pouring smoke. We moved into second, trailing Stommelen and Grohs by just under two minutes. Our brake pads, which had lasted the distance, were now nearly worn through. Brian could barely extend his leg enough to make the pedal work.

And so it finished. Bobby Rahal, who came in fifth, still had a mathematical chance of the championship—he would have to win pole position and each of the three remaining races, while Brian scored no points—but he clearly did not intend to pursue it. Brian and the Lola were champions.

Two weeks after Elkhart Lake the Cooke-Woods team raced again, with Brian winning in a brilliant drive at Road Atlanta. Two weeks after *that,* Ralph Kent Cooke co-drove with Brian at Pocono, the pair taking second in a rain-shortened event. And at Daytona, the final race of the season, Brian was once again second.

From its Laguna Seca debut through Daytona, the Lola had been entered in 10 races, winning 5 and finishing second in 5. Years from now people will look back into the record book and say to themselves, "Five wins and five seconds? Boy, they must have had it easy," forgetting that the Lola was a prototype that was being sorted as the season went along; that midway through the season, a whole new team had to be brought in to prepare the car; and that every single race was an exercise in coming from behind against more powerful cars. And forgetting, too, that strangely battered wheel nut on Brian Redman's mantelpiece. . . . The long summer twilight was starting to fade. John and the men had disassembled the canopy. The car, polished and checked once again, was in the transporter.

It was time to celebrate. At Road America, this means driving over for dinner at Siebkens, about three miles away. Siebkens is a hotel—they may even call it a resort hotel, because of the lake across the road and the tennis courts that are out back somewhere. The place looks like it's 100 years old, and before dinner a line of racers forms on the stairs to use the single phone at the top. You eat in an L-shaped enclosed porch, and long tables accommodate entire racing teams. Food is served by lovely young girls in red-and-white-striped dresses, and naturally everyone has plenty to drink. Conversation is out of the question unless you shout.

In fact, the atmosphere at Siebkens is so agreeable that you might go there even if you had *not* had a successful day at the track, knowing you would be treated exactly as if you had won. Which is how it happened that David Hobbs, whose BMW had expired early in the going, was dining there with his wife, Margaret, and their friends.

From where the Cooke-Woods contingent sat with Brian at the head of the table, the BMW table was out of sight, around the corner of the L. So I did not see David approaching with a large pie until he was directly behind Brian. Even then I might have been able to warn Brian, but David's expression—as serene and luminous as an angel's—caught me off guard.

"Well, old boy," David began, his voice quiet yet clearly audible in the din, "I'd like to congratulate you on the championship . . ."

Brian started to turn around, smiling, and received the pie full in the face. A roar went up from the room as David calmly continued the job, grinding the pie into Brian's hair.

Brian remained motionless, but when David was finished and the clamor subsided for a moment, Brian stood up.

"Lemon meringue," announced the new champion.

This article was written as Brian's pro career was tapering off but before he became the doyen of the vintage-car world. Although it was a worrisome time for him, he never lost his sense of humor. I suppose that surviving his frightful accidents, which I describe here, gave him a certain resiliency, but I believe there's an innate cheerfulness in his DNA. In any case, I feel lucky to count this remarkable man as a friend.

Recently, I had the honor of writing a profile of Brian for the annual Road Racing Drivers Club banquet; the text can be found in the third section of this book.

Brian Redman—Racing's Invisible Champion

ROAD & TRACK, FEBRUARY 2000

The guard at the gate has the most perfectly polished black shoes you'll ever see, and just now they reflect the palm trees and clear, cerulean sky of Florida's east coast. Beyond the gate lies a world of freshly cut lawns, uniformed men tending bright flower beds, and understated houses, each with a pool out back and a Seville or Town Car in the garage. A championship golf course winds through the sprawling property, affording glimpses of greens and fairways, along with golf carts that move in silent packs through the moist, hot air.

Brian Redman seems out of place living here; he does not play golf, and behind his garage door is an MG TC. But then Brian has never fit any stereotype.

He is often described as "underrated," or as "racing's best-kept secret," because his career doesn't happen to be neatly defined by the events that get big publicity. For example, he has never raced at Indy or in the Daytona 500, and he ran only a dozen grand prix. In long-distance racing, he was one of the best (he drove for teams that won four

I have written more about Brian than I have about any other driver. I am a great fan of his, and I hope some of that comes through. He is warm, funny, and very, very fast.

Manufacturers Championships), yet because he was usually paired with headliners such as Ickx and Siffert, he was regarded as a sort of second banana. Many of his finest races, and three consecutive championships, came in a series—Formula 5000—that has been defunct for more than 20 years. And his recent wins have been in vintage racing, where the focus is on the cars, not the drivers.

He is tweedy and avuncular, tanned in a leathery sort of way, and his presence puts you immediately at ease. He is great company, delighting in absurdities such as a trick in which he dangles a spoon from his nose. Phil Hill was surprised recently when Brian called with no agenda other than to see how he was doing. He has a cheerful buoyancy that makes him seem much younger than 62. He moved to the United States from England 19 years ago, but he has not lost his accent, and it is wonderful to hear Brian entertaining a crowd with one of his many stories: "Herr Redman, remember your crash in ze Targa Florio? All that was left was a hole burned in ze road, with a crankshaft lying in ze bottom of it! Ha, ha!" He was born on March 9, 1937, in Colne, Lancashire. His family was in the retail grocery business. He was sent away to boarding school in Wales at the age of eight, where the Welsh kids, resentful of the young Englishman, took every opportunity to bully and humiliate him, actually stoning him in the driveway. He put in three years at a catering college in Blackpool, then a stretch in the army, which brought an innate dislike of authority to a boil. His grandfather had a small business manufacturing and selling mops, which Brian inherited when the older man died in 1962. His grandfather also had a love of racing, and Brian inherited that, too. His first race was Easter Monday, 1959, in a boosted Morris Oxford woodie that doubled as the mop company's delivery van.

Brian was hooked but unable to afford good equipment, and it wasn't until 1965 that he finally landed a ride—in an E-type Jaguar—in which he could show what he could do. Often driving far over his head, he won 15 of 16 races. The Jag was followed with rides in a Lola T70 and a smattering of Formula 2. It was the big time. (Or almost; Brian remembers that after a particularly dangerous race at Spa, his car owner noticed some empty cans lying around the pits and asked him to pick them up so he could get a refund!)

At the end of 1967, however, he got a break that was the real thing: Ace team manager John Wyer paired him with Jacky Ickx in the Manufacturers Championship at Kyalami and, when they won, Wyer signed Brian for the 1968 season. Meanwhile, Cooper hired him for Formula One. Brian was too old at the age of 31 to generate the buzz of a "rising star," but that didn't matter; life looked good. He bought a house for his family, which consisted of his wife Marion and their young son James (their daughter Charlotte was soon to be born), and he looked forward to the season. It started well, with wins at Brands Hatch and Spa for Wyer, and a third place in the Spanish GP for Cooper.

But the spring of 1968 was not like other years. Jim Clark, Ludovico Scarfiotti, Mike Spence, and Jo Schlesser were killed. Suddenly no driver felt safe.

In June, Brian had a big crash of his own—at Spa, in the Belgian GP. He was cresting the hill after Eau Rouge at 150 mph when the Cooper's right front wishbone collapsed. He hit the guardrail head-on, rolled over into a corner worker's car, and then hit another car. His right arm was crushed. The doctors were ready to amputate but changed their minds at the last minute, installing a lot of bolts and steel plates instead. But the arm refused to heal, and as the summer turned into fall, Brian felt a sense of growing panic. Was his nascent career finished?

Porsche had been impressed by his drives with Wyer, and they had offered him a ride for 1969. Brian became desperate to be ready for the first race, the 24 Hours of Daytona. With six weeks to go, he underwent a bone graft. The operation was a success, but at Daytona he still had to steer and shift with his left hand. He had no idea how he would make it through the race—until his problem was solved when the team's five 908s all failed early.

After the race Porsche team manager Rico Steinmann asked him to choose between being the number-one driver in his own car, or driving with Jo Siffert as number two. He went with Siffert, believing "I'd win more often that way." He was right; with Brian's arm fully recovered, the pair won 5 out of 10 races, and delivered Porsche's first Manufacturers Championship, but the price was that Siffert got most of the credit.

For 1970, Porsche made a deal with John Wyer to run their new, very fast 917s, and Brian rejoined the team. Wyer kept Siffert and Redman together, and they had another big year, while Porsche won its second championship. But more drivers had been killed the previous year, and one of them, John Woolfe, died in a 917.

"I was terrified of the early versions of that car," Brian says. "The frames were always cracking, and you never really felt secure in one. At Le Mans, it would do over 235 mph, but it changed lanes without warning, and you had to steer all the way down the straight."

Funerals were becoming routine.

"For Gerhard Mitter's, they had us carrying the casket—wearing our driver's uniforms," Brian recalls. "Afterward, I was crying, and someone asked if I had known Mitter that well. 'No,' I said. 'I'm crying for me!'" Brian was convinced he could be next.

He had been offered a job at a BMW dealership in Johannesburg, and, after agonizing over the decision, he resolved to quit racing. At age 33, he left England, taking his family with him.

He thought he was ready to begin a new life in South Africa, but his plans soon went awry. He disliked the routine work in the dealership, and he worried about apartheid. He entered the Springbok series as a sort of farewell to the sport, but then he won all six races—and realized retiring had been a very big mistake. Two months after leaving England, he was back, along with his family and belongings.

"In a sense," he recalls, "my attempt to retire taught me that not racing just wasn't a choice. Not for me then. It also taught me to value persistence, to realize how often things come around if you don't give up."

John Wyer had hired a replacement, but he wanted Brian for the Targa Florio. Brian's "comeback" lasted 20 miles. The 908's steering broke, and the car struck a concrete post, catching fire before Brian could get out. "I heard somebody screaming," he remembers, "and it was a while before I realized it was me. It was the same as at Spa; I didn't feel any pain at first. The body is amazing that way. Something in you rises up and blocks everything out." The pain would come soon enough, however, with a doctor taking a stiff brush and scraping Brian's face raw.

For the second time in just three years, he would have to make a comeback. This time, however, he would have no doubts about his commitment to racing, and for the next six years he would be at the top of his game, rolling up wins of such quality—and quantity—that if it had been anyone else, he would have been hailed as a superstar.

His face had healed by the fall of 1971, and although he was badly scarred, Brian was eager to drive again as soon as possible, and persuaded BRM to lend him a car for the Interseries races at Hockenheim and Imola. He won both. The Ferrari team was at Imola, where Brian lapped the field in the rain, and they offered him a seat on their long-distance team for 1972.

Ferrari had tried to hire him four years earlier, but after a trial race at the Nürburgring, Brian had seen that the team put constant pressure on its drivers (for example, in practice they had told him he was 10th when he was actually 4th), and he knew he would try to respond and that the ride could be a nightmare. "When I turned them down, they said, 'Nobody ever gets a second chance with Ferrari.' But here they were, asking me again," Brian recalls.

This time, former driver Peter Schetty was the team manager, and Brian accepted, joining a lineup that included Ronnie Peterson, Jacky Ickx, Mario Andretti, and Clay Regazzoni. Redman proved to be as fast as any of them, and in two years he won seven races with Ferrari's 312.

At the end of 1972, Brian signed with Lola importer Carl Haas and Jim Hall, of Chaparral fame, to drive their Formula 5000 car, which was essentially an F1 car with a monstrous 460 bhp Chevy. The deal was his first in the United States, and it would lead to his eventual move here.

In 1973 he missed some of the events due to date conflicts with the Ferrari program—but he still won five races in seven starts, and almost stole the championship from Jody Scheckter. In 1974 and 1975, Brian defeated Mario Andretti, and in 1976 he beat Al Unser—for his third consecutive championship. These successes came at the expense of men who would go on to become World Champions—or, in Unser's case, to win Indy four times. Along the way, Brian won almost half the races—including the first race at Long Beach—and blew off two other future World Champions, Alan Jones and James Hunt. (He also fitted in some races for BMW, winning Daytona and Sebring.)

Like Rick Mears, he was an unerring judge of pace. His gift for making tricky passes meant he was rarely held up in traffic, and as far as I know, he never blocked anyone. He also possessed an intuitive technical savvy that enabled him to set up his car in just a few laps and nurse it along if something was wrong. He could dig very deep when he had to. Fast, tough, levelheaded, confident—yet fully aware of how suddenly things could go wrong; Brian Redman was a great driver in full bloom in a series that offered some of the best road racing ever seen in this country.

Formula 5000, however, was dying. Many theories were advanced (one even blamed Redman's journeyman image, implying that the series needed a Big Winner who was more glamorous), but for 1977 new rules called for Formula 5000 cars to race with full bodywork, thereby transforming them into ersatz Can-Am cars. This led directly to Brian's third big crash.

In May, at Saint-Jovite, the fendered Lola caught some air under the nose at 160 mph and took off. It landed upside down, collapsing the rollbar. Brian's neck was broken, along with his sternum, his shoulder, and three ribs. His brain was bruised. After his Targa Florio fire, he had been taken to the wrong hospital; this time, the ambulance blew a tire at 100 mph and crashed. Brian spent the summer strapped down on his back, his head kept motionless by weights suspended from bolts drilled into his skull.

Eight years before, when Brian returned to Spa for the first time after his accident there, he had made a point of setting fastest lap, "because I didn't want to be beaten by whatever fate had dealt me." Once again, fate had to be shown who was boss, and Brian entered the first race he could. This was Sebring, 1978. In a nondescript Porsche 935, with Charles Mendez and Bob Garretson co-driving, he won. Only this time, his comeback hit an unexpected dead end.

Brian was now 41, and after Sebring he had trouble getting rides. One year went by, then another. In 1980, he emigrated to the United States, and to make ends meet he went to work for Carl Haas, selling Lolas. Depressed by the bleakness of his future, he realized he would have to create an opportunity of his own. With his eye on a car that could exploit new IMSA rules designed to end the Porsche dominance of the GTX class, he managed to arrange a partnership between Roy Woods and Ralph Kent Cooke to run a Lola T600 in the 1981 season.

The car was bright yellow, suggesting that after four dark years the sun was once again shining on Brian Redman. And it was—although at the very first race he came close to disaster when a rear hub nut worked loose, breaking the safety clip and leaving the car lurching all over the track. Brian was falling back through the pack when the rotation of the wheel began to tighten the nut back up. He won. And he would win another four races, along with the championship.

I happened to co-drive with Brian at Elkhart Lake, where he clinched the championship, and at the party afterward he was at his inimitable best as he went from table to table, finishing off any drinks he could get his hands on, all the while with a spoon hanging miraculously from his nose.

It was a bittersweet moment because Brian knew the team was being disbanded. The Lola was followed by a murky patchwork of rides, a few isolated wins, and stretches of semiretirement. There was another discouraging attempt to work at a dealership.

But even as Brian's racing career was unraveling, a previously obscure form of the sport—vintage racing—was beginning to flourish. The vintage world was made up of people who really knew their racing history, and the more they knew, the more often Brian's name came up. He was an expert on the very cars they were interested in: GT40s, 917s, Lolas,

Lotuses, Ferraris—he'd driven them all! And he had an inexhaustible supply of anecdotes, which made him the perfect after-dinner speaker. All at once, Brian was being reincarnated, this time as a Major Hero, and he responded with zest.

Seeing that there were vintage drivers who wanted more track time and a less hectic atmosphere, he created a limited-membership club called Targa Sixty Six, which is now in its eighth year. Next, working with his son James, who showed an organizational flair, Brian organized a series for Merrill Lynch, including the Merrill Lynch / Brian Redman International Challenge, which last year attracted more than 500 cars and 40,000 spectators to Road America. A Brian Redman book has appeared. Brian Redman hats are hot items at concession stands. Best of all, most weekends include Mr. Redman himself winning the big race—with the very same Chevron B19 he had run in the Springbok Series when he won six in a row and realized that his plan to retire would never work.

Brian has been racing now for 40 years—a life that has brought full measures of success and pain. Recently, he was dining with Marion on the outdoor patio of a restaurant near their home. It was evening, and the heat of the Florida day had cooled. Marion was in a reflective mood.

"All in all, Brian," she said, "you've been very lucky."

This article was written ten years after Mark's death and three years after I had retired. I was missing racing, and fully understood why Mark had come out of retirement when Roger Penske offered him a full season in Formula One.

Racing was very different then; there was still glory in taking risks, and drivers who were killed were considered to have died a heroic death. Today, getting killed is just stupid.

Every year, I go to Bill Warner's Amelia Island Concours and meet up with drivers who were my opponents—the bad guys—when we were racing. We start swapping stories, and suddenly I have a new friend.

What I'd give to talk to Mark again . . .

Magnificent Obsession
ROAD & TRACK, JUNE 1992

Twenty years ago, on May 27, 1972, a driver with a degree in mechanical engineering from Brown University won the Indianapolis 500. His name: Mark Donohue.

It was a time of change, with technology transforming the American racing scene, often with Donohue himself in the vanguard. He was something new, a gunslinger who also happened to have designed the gun. He was admired, feared, or emulated, depending on your perspective. You knew, seeing him with his briefcase, his charts and formulas, that racing would never be the same. When you heard he was working so hard that he was sleeping on the floor of the shop, you knew the days of racing as a romantic hobby were over. He made you look at yourself and wonder how committed you really were.

He was very fast, but he didn't have true virtuosity to fall back on. In the heat of battle, when you were so close to him that you and he were doing the same things at the same moment, you could feel him working for every inch. There was nobility in his effort. He showed how a man can be lifted far above himself by the sheer force of his will. People were drawn to him because of that, and few rivals begrudged him his victories. You could sense the strain; you felt he was reaching beyond himself out of some dark duty, and it seemed that no matter what he accomplished, he couldn't rest.

Indy, for example, had been a long-cherished goal, but when he won it, he couldn't savor it because the victory hadn't come on his terms. As that May had unfolded, he had been unable to find a competitive setup for the chassis of his car, a McLaren-Offy. Having dominated the race in a similar car the year before, until the transmission failed, he was bewildered. With time running out, his car owner, Roger Penske, asked that he adopt the chassis settings of Mark's close rivals, the McLaren factory team. At the same time, Penske's Offy engines were flawed, and Mark had to go to Parnelli Jones, his bitter adversary in the Trans-Am, to rent an engine. To Mark, this was like a gunslinger who has to borrow his gun, and the bullets, from his enemies.

Things got worse. In the race, Mark was left in the dust—first by Bobby Unser's Eagle, then by his own teammate, Gary Bettenhausen. It wasn't until the star-crossed Bettenhausen suffered a pinhole leak in his car's header tank that Mark inherited the lead, just 12 laps from the end.

To him, it was a victory he backed into, and less than an hour after the checkered flag, with the crew beginning to pack up, Mark volunteered to drive the team's timer, Judy Stropus, to the airport, and on the way barely mentioned the race. He could not have known that his race average of 162.962 mph would become an Indy record that would stand for 11 years, or that he had laid the cornerstone for a dynasty (Penske's team has won, to date, seven more Indy 500s). Clearly he could not have foreseen that this win would be publicly regarded as the high point of his career, bringing him considerable celebrity—or that in little more than three years, on August 19, 1975, he would be dead.

I knew Mark Donohue and raced with him. But I was seven years younger, and most of the time I thought more in terms of trying to follow in his footsteps than of beating him. In a race at Watkins Glen in 1967, I was behind Mark when Bob Bondurant had the big accident that ended

Mark died well before his time, but he wasn't a romantic figure like James Dean or Buddy Holly. He was practical, and always thought through the consequences—which made his death all the more bitter.

his career. The yellow flags were waving, and Mark slowed. I slowed even more, then got a run on him and passed him for the lead just as we exited the yellow-flag zone. I remember the look of utter disgust on his face as I swept by, and I thought, *Uh-oh, I shouldn't have done that.*

The next year I was his teammate for several Trans-Ams when he won the championship for Chevrolet. And the day he won Indy, I was fifth. To me it was business as usual: Mark winning, me trailing along behind, thinking maybe one day, my time would come.

But then he was killed.

My wife-to-be, Ellen, and I were watching TV in her apartment in Los Angeles when we heard the news. In those years, a lot of the drivers we knew had been killed, but I always found a way to rationalize it and keep going. This was different. I knew Mark was better than I was, and smarter. Luckier, even. If it could happen to him, it could happen to me. I couldn't escape that logic.

I turned to Ellen, and she looked at me and said, "You're going to quit, aren't you?" And I did quit. I continued racing sedans, but I stopped driving open-wheelers. The light at the end of the tunnel was out.

The point was often made that Mark didn't look like a race driver. He had a roundish face and, for many years, a crew cut. Until the last two years of his life, he seemed a bit overweight. Nor did his upbringing hint at his future. His father was a patent attorney, a very proper Easterner. Mark and his two sisters were reared as good Catholics in Summit, New Jersey. When he was six, Mark contracted polio but recovered fully. After graduating from Brown in 1959, he worked for Raybestos in Passaic, then had a stint selling industrial dust collectors. Neither job held much appeal, and he certainly was not ready to settle down in a regular job.

He loved practical jokes. Mark and his friend Burge Hulett had an arrangement whereby, upon spotting the approach of the other's car, each would veer into the left lane, thus passing on the "wrong" side of the road, leaving their passengers breathless.

And then there was his interest in cars. His early racing efforts had shown he had driving talent. While a senior in college, he entered his first event, a hillclimb, and won it with his two-year-old Corvette. In 1961 he bought an Elva Courier and battled with another young Easterner, Peter Revson, for the Sports Car Club of America's divisional championship in E Production. Donohue won, but the success failed to generate any momentum. Unable to raise enough money, he raced very little in 1962 and 1963.

In 1964 he was hired by Jack Griffith, a Long Island Ford dealer, as chief engineer for Griffith's ill-fated car-building venture. Mark was 27, apparently just another guy out there trying to get something going that would keep him around cars. And yet, despite the cherubic look and only sporadic success, certain people were beginning to believe that Mark Donohue was special.

One of these was the established pro Walt Hansgen, who arranged for Mark to drive with him in Texas oilman John Mecom's Ferrari 250 LM at Sebring in 1965. The same year, a wealthy young sportsman named Malcolm Starr gave Mark rides in a Mustang and a Lotus 20B Formula Junior. When Mark won divisional championships in both cars, Hansgen was able to persuade Ford to hire his young protégé for its team in 1966. Hansgen and Donohue drove their GT40 to third place at Daytona and second at Sebring.

Just weeks later, testing for Le Mans, Hansgen was killed. It is a considerable irony that it was at Hansgen's funeral that Roger Penske broached the subject of Mark's driving for him. Jay Signore, at that time a driver (he is IROC's head man today), had also recommended Mark, and as Roger recalls, "Mark was known to have a methodical approach, and he was willing to commit to working for me full-time, which counted for a lot."

Penske at that point did not really have a team. He had ace mechanic Karl Kainhofer installed in a small shop with a Lola T70 he had bought from John Mecom. The Lola was ready to go by midsummer, in time for the US Road Racing Championship (USRRC), precursor to the Can-Am, at Watkins Glen. John Hilton, who was managing his father's team (with driver Charlie Parsons), recalls the moment. "Four of us were battling for the championship, all running McLarens. Then off rolled this Lola, and it was absolutely immaculate; nobody had ever seen anything like it. It was so sleek and clean. And Mark just jumped into the car and smoked us all in qualifying." In the race, he crested a blind rise and crashed into another car that was spinning across the track. The Lola was destroyed.

Roger persuaded his sponsor, the Sun Oil Company, to advance money against the contract, and a new car was purchased. A few weeks later the Penske/Donohue combination won the USRRC in Kent, Washington. It was the beginning of an era.

My brief stint with the team came in the summer of 1968, four races in a second Camaro to Mark's. Our opposition was Ford's team of George Follmer and Parnelli Jones, and I was brought in because Roger thought George and Parnelli might gang up on Mark. I was the team's insurance policy.

In my first race, Bridgehampton, we were headed up the straight on the first lap, with Mark leading and me off to his right, the Mustangs on our bumpers, when I saw Mark reach for his rearview mirror and twist it up, sending a signal to George and Parnelli that he didn't care what they had in mind.

Those were tough races, three hours long. I would sweat so much my earplugs would wash out, and I'd be deafened by half distance, and for two days afterward. When I called home after a race, Mark would have to talk to my mom for me because I couldn't hear. The steering was brutally heavy because he used so much caster. You came out of every turn oversteering, which I found was very fast until I got tired.

But Mark never tired. Very few people knew it, but he lifted weights and ran, long before this was fashionable. He looked soft, but he was made of iron.

He believed that Dan Gurney, Parnelli Jones, and a few other drivers were faster than he was, but that only meant he had to try harder and plan more elaborately to beat them. Willpower. Duty. And engineering. He had terrific confidence in his engineering. Cause and effect. Thinking that was linear and sequential. And it was seductive how well it worked. He'd say that out of 10 things he'd try, only 3 would help, but with Roger footing the bills for a new skidpad at the shop and test sessions at tracks all over the country, Mark had the luxury of trying almost everything he could think up.

And he had a very curious nature. Finding loopholes in the rules, the quest for what he and Roger called the "unfair advantage," became obsessive. One week they sped up refueling with a 25-foot-high tower. Another week they squeezed more into the tank by cooling the fuel with dry ice. Chevrolet engineers such as Don Cox and Chuck Cantwell, at first only a phone call away, soon were working for the team full-time. Terms like *friction circle, roll couple,* and *center of pressure* were in everyday use. Mark's briefcase bulged. Hanging in the air was the quest for some still-unknown relationship between science and sport. At times Mark seemed to have come from somewhere outside of racing and was blasting through it, headed out the other side.

The team was something entirely new. Partly it was The Look. The gleaming, pinstriped car, elegant in the deep blue of Penske's patrician sponsor, Sunoco, was the center of the universe. Then add the matching uniforms, the custom slantback trucks (which Mark designed), the racks of spares, the Learjet. In time, other teams would find the money and emulate The Look. What they could not attain was The Attitude. This was more than commitment and dedication; it was an approach to racing as a condition of war.

From the outset, a synergism existed between Mark and Roger that enabled each to submerge his own monumental ego for the good of the common cause. Life in the team was a hermetic cocoon. Events of the day—Vietnam, Watergate—went virtually unnoticed. Young Al Holbert, working as an apprentice mechanic, was so drawn into this special world that he even changed his handwriting, patterning it after Mark's. The team had its own code. Roger was "The Captain"; George

Follmer, "The Fumbler." Post-race celebrations included everyone in the team and an open bar (drinks were "shooters"), but at midnight "the meter went back to zero"; the trucks would pull out of the parking lot, usually with Mark driving one of them, and begin the trip back to home base in Reading, Pennsylvania.

"Get the job done" was another phrase we heard a lot. Roger drilled into the team that you could be at the top, but the minute you believed you had it made, you were already sliding downhill. Roger didn't have to motivate Mark, however. Mark was his own harshest critic. Out-qualified by Jerry Titus at Saint-Jovite in Canada, he went to the hotel bar, ordered a double bourbon, and then another, gulping them both down, and without a word to anyone he headed off for bed. The next day he blew Titus's doors off.

Mostly, life was good. Practical jokes were in high gear. John Hilton, now with the team, returned from a date at one a.m., keeping the light out so as not to wake Mark, and found his bed soaked in honey and Mark chuckling in the dark. It was unwise to stop at an intersection with Mark behind; you would be pushed out into traffic. In the races, he would play tricks with his brake lights, which he had wired to a hand-operated switch. A naturally shy person, he had the team, which he could trust, as an extended family. Secrets were the order of the day, and outsiders were made to feel uneasy. When you went to greet Mark, he'd extend his hand, then snatch it away, leaving you grasping thin air.

Thin air was about all the rest of us were left to work with. In 1967 Mark became USRRC champion, winning 6 of 8 races. In 1968 he was USRRC champion again, winning 5 of 8, and he delivered the Trans-Am championship for Chevrolet, winning 10 of 13. (Note that in an era when a 50 percent breakdown rate was typical, Mark finished virtually every race he entered, thanks to Karl Kainhofer and the team's other super mechanics, plus bulletproof engines from Traco.) In 1969 Mark repeated his Trans-Am success, winning 6 of 12, and another championship for Penske and Chevrolet.

And then, about the time he won Indy in 1972, things began to unravel.

Basically, Mark was overworked. Other drivers could maintain heavy racing schedules because during the week they could rest, but for Mark the week meant 20-hour workdays at the shop. He wanted it that way, wanted to be involved in every decision, and the team relied on him. But gradually it became too much. The team's success enabled Roger to make more deals, bigger deals (like the huge undertaking for American Motors in the Trans-Am), and Mark became crushed by his responsibilities.

He had to make too many decisions, too fast, and he didn't have time to think things through. Often he had to rely purely on instinct, which is anathema to an engineer. Exhaustion alternated with the adrenaline rushes of the race weekends. He began sleeping on the floor of the shop. His relationship with his wife, Sue, self-destructed, and from this point on he would see less than ever of his two young sons, David and Michael. When a friend, George Lysle, persuaded him to let International Management Group handle his personal affairs, Mark brought two shoeboxes of unpaid bills to their office, his personal life in chaos.

In the early years he and Roger had been roped together like mountaineers, each dependent on the other, but now Roger was moving ahead in a world of his own, building an industrial empire, amassing a personal fortune. Roger and Mark had always seemed about the same age, but now Roger was a young corporate executive with an unlimited future, whereas Mark was an aging driver starting to run out of time.

Judy Stropus was very close to Mark during this period, and she recalls that he became terribly insecure, convinced that Roger could replace him with A. J. Foyt, or anyone else he might want.

Much of this was abstract and might have blown over in time. But five weeks after Indy, on July 3, he was testing his Can-Am Porsche, the 917/10, at Road Atlanta and got airborne at 160 mph, did two cartwheels, and wound up in the hospital. His legs were broken, and to control the pain he was kept on drugs, which affected his memory and produced a sense of dislocation.

His return to racing saw him winning again by September, but now he was acutely aware of the price at which his success was achieved.

The winter of 1972–73 brought frequent trips to Germany to test the Porsche 917/30. Mike Knepper, whose article for *R & T* (August 1974) captured with chilling accuracy the grimness of this period, quotes Mark as saying, "When it snowed in Germany and we couldn't test, the boredom became intolerable. After I'd read everything I could find in English, I'd just sit in my room and stare."

Indy approached again. Still agonizing over having won "by default" the previous year, Mark persuaded Roger to buy him an Eagle to race against the McLarens of the factory team and his own teammate, Bettenhausen. This was an effort to rehabilitate his sense of himself as an engineer, but from the beginning, he was in trouble. To sort out the Eagle his way would take more time than he had.

Mark could not generate self-esteem from anything outside of racing, and he hit a desperate low. Without telling anyone, he made the decision to quit racing. He managed to qualify third, and was running third at 91 laps when the engine failed, but this did not change his mind. During the delay caused by Swede Savage's fatal crash, writer Charles Fox approached Mark, noticed that he was ashen, and asked how he was doing. "Just trying to keep my ass in one piece and make a buck" came the terse reply. In Mark's mind, his career was over.

It must have been bittersweet, therefore, when the rest of the 1973 season produced two major championships: in the Can-Am (he won six races in a row), and in the first-ever International Race of Champions series (he won three of four races). But despite the success, people close to him ceased calling him "Captain Nice," and referred to him instead as "Dark Monohue."

In retirement, he became president of Penske racing, and his day-to-day responsibilities were very much as before, except that now the satisfaction of driving the car belonged to someone else. Brian Redman, who drove for the team in 1974, recalls that Mark was distant and jealous; Mark admitted that "having someone else in the car is like someone sleeping with my wife."

For the first time in eight years, however, Mark had some semblance of a private life. He bought a boat and moved into a bachelor pad. Most significantly, he was in love. Eden White was an Atlanta socialite, seven years younger than Mark, a delicate beauty who spent her summers modeling and her winters skiing in Vail. They had met when Mark was hospitalized in Atlanta, and now their times together seemed to point to a life beyond racing—except that Mark could not fully envision how such a life could be. He was not easing gracefully into the role of team manager, nor did his salary (about a third of what he had earned driving) seem adequate. He started a business that sold racing accessories, but this only poked along. Drivers need time to get over racing, to find that another life can be fulfilling, too. Mark never gave himself the chance.

Less than a year after Mark retired, Roger offered him a ride in Formula One. Mark wanted to be challenged again, to feel the force of his own willpower pulling him forward. He wanted Eden to know that Mark Donohue. "He wanted to show he could do it all again," Roger recalls. Mark came out of retirement for the last two grand prix of 1974, and that winter he and Eden married and had a hurried honeymoon in Jamaica. He began the 1975 Formula One season as a 38-year-old rookie, the oldest driver on the grid.

I last saw him on the morning of the Dutch Grand Prix, eight weeks before he was killed. The season had been a disaster, a litany of crashes and poor placings. I found him crouched on the upper ramp in the transporter, the rain beating on the roof just inches away. This time he did not refuse my hand.

"Roger won't talk to me," he said, obviously in anguish, and I was miserable for him. But I didn't blame Roger; he was busy entertaining the sponsors who had paid for the Penske/Donohue magic and were not getting any.

In Austria, at the Österreichring, he was running the car on full tanks during practice the morning of the race when he understeered off into a catch fence. A post struck him on the helmet. He returned to the pits and talked to the crew. He seemed unhurt, but it was fate's turn to play a practical joke because, in fact, Mark's brain was hemorrhaging. Soon he said he had a headache. Next, he collapsed. He was flown to a hospital and operated on, but it was too late.

His heirs contended that the crash was caused by a tire failure, and a lawsuit was brought against Goodyear, resulting in a $12 million settlement. In death, Mark had made his family rich. He died just as a new era of safer cars was dawning, cars that his own engineering expertise helped to bring into existence. In fact, he is, to date, the last Indy winner to be killed racing. He was the prototype for the totally dedicated driver, and when I see Rick Mears today, I often think of Mark.

In hindsight, it can be seen that his return to racing was a tragic mistake, but at the time it made sense to him, and he was responding to the instinct that had made him great, as well as, possibly, that sense of dark duty that seemed to drive him. At the end, he became a hapless victim in a freak crash. Does that diminish him? I don't think so; it only underscores how human he really was.

Recently, I asked John Hilton how he remembers Mark, and he said, "Laughing. We always seemed to do a lot of laughing." I will tell you that John Hilton was crying as he said that. As Roger says today, "Mark wasn't flashy, but he put the numbers on the board." And made a lot of people realize that the racing world would never be quite the same without him.

Jim McKay's job brought him into contact with many people in the world of sport, and the man he admired the most was Phil Hill. The feeling was mutual. Jim could do imitations of Phil that were so accurate that when Phil would tell a story, you thought he was imitating Jim.

Phil heard I had Parkinson's and he took to calling me from time to time, to ask how I was doing. Then one day he called and said, "I've got your thing." I did my best to cheer him up, but what neither of us knew then was how fast his particular form of the disease would kill him. The two friends died within three months of each other. Two lights going out—and leaving the world a little darker.

A Man like No Other
ROAD & TRACK, JULY 2011

W ho was Phil Hill? The first American Formula One World Champion—that's the short answer. He won the title exactly 50 years ago, and we celebrate that now. But a tragedy accompanied his championship, casting a shadow across the achievement that is the cornerstone of his fame; and in any case, the title *World Champion*—glorious as it is—too conveniently pigeonholes this exceedingly complex man.

I met him in the lobby of a Sebring hotel two years before he won the championship. I was 14 and already an avid racing fan. When I saw him I must have frozen in my tracks, because he walked over to me and said, "Can I help?"

As the years went by I came to know him as a friend, but I never entirely lost that original sense of awe; he was a hero to me then and remains a hero to me today, three years after his death.

It was his driving that came the closest to defining him. It revealed the nerves that sidelined him for months with an ulcer. It showed the sacrifices he was willing to make, like doing thousands of deep knee

Phil was one of my first heroes in racing, and it never occurred to me that someday he would become a friend.

bends so he'd have the strength to push harder on the brakes. It exposed the profound doubts he had about racing's violence and danger. (Denise McCluggage described him as Hamlet in a helmet.) Racing taught him that he didn't compete so much by choice as from a compulsive need to do what he did best, to answer the call of the forces that drew him to the sport. And it was driving that led him to Monza on September 10, 1961, for the most important day of his professional life.

The year 1961 was Ferrari's year. There had been a massive rules change, and the English teams like Cooper and Lotus weren't ready; Ferrari was, and from the beginning it was clear that a Ferrari driver—either Hill or his teammate Wolfgang von Trips—would wind up champion.

ABOVE: "Gentlemen, start your engines!"

RIGHT: Barely 22, I'm about to become the youngest American to drive at Le Mans. My Bizzarrini is in the background. We didn't finish, but for me it was the beginning of a chapter in my life—driving at Le Mans. I did it ten times, and every year was different—the race had changed, and so had I.

ABOVE: Bridgehampton, USRRC, 1967. Upside down in the car, you're in the dark, and afraid of fire. This crash happened early in the race, so the McLaren had nearly full tanks. I was extremely grateful to the course workers for getting me out in a hurry.

RIGHT: The Corkscrew, Laguna Seca, 1969, Eagle-Chevrolet. This was my first win in F5000. The week before, I had totaled the all-new Eagle we'd spent the winter preparing. My chief mechanic, Jack McCormack, worked around the clock to get this car together.

ABOVE: Le Mans, 1970. Ronnie Bucknum (seen here) and I drove this long-tailed NART Ferrari 512 S. It went 248 mph, but the Porsche 917s were even faster.

ABOVE: Another win? There were so many, I can't remember which was which.

RIGHT: The lime-green Dodge Challenger prepared by Ray Caldwell's Autodynamics for 1970. This was the great year of the Trans-Am, and I was lucky to be part of it.

OPPOSITE: Mike Parkes and I won the Prototype class with this NART Ferrari at Daytona in 1970. We were both tall and the car was very low. Our fabricator, Wayne Sparling, put a bubble in the roof.

RIGHT: I created the design for my helmet. The stripes are meant to suggest the American flag.

BELOW: Le Mans, 1971. I drove the NART Ferrari 512 M. Ellen and I were on our first date, and she took this picture.

ABOVE: Le Mans, 1971. I held the lap record for several hours. Tony Adamowicz and I finished third—again, the highest-placed Ferrari.

LEFT: Driving an F1 Surtees, USGP, 1971. My proudest moment in racing.

RIGHT: Seattle, 1971. Wait until we get the Goodyears on this thing.

BELOW: Indianapolis, Eagle-Offy, 1972. A day when everything—absolutely everything—went right.

ABOVE: The BMW mechanics were taking a casual approach to preparing the car, so I knew something was up.

LEFT: Road racers were naturals at Indy. I had driven the fast turns at Le Mans, so felt comfortable at the Brickyard. More importantly, I had a great chief mechanic in Jack McCormack. We qualified seventh, and finished fifth; I was the fastest rookie in the field.

ABOVE: Le Mans, 1977. We worked in a garage right across the square from the hotel.

LEFT: When Mario has your patch sewn on his suit, it costs you big bucks; on my suit—well, not so much.

OPPOSITE: In 1975, with my mother at Sebring. Sixteen years before, she had brought me to the race for the first time, and now I was just a few hours away from winning it.

RIGHT: Elkhart Lake, 1981, driving the Lola T600 I shared with Brian Redman. This was a *Road & Track* photo shoot the day after the race. Ellen is lying on her back somewhere down near the pedals to get this perspective.

BELOW: Paul Newman and I testing Bob Sharp's turbo-charged Datsun at Stewart Air Force Base.

ABOVE: Lola T600 at Elkhart Lake, 1981.

LEFT: The start/finish tower at Lime Rock, which I designed with my brother, David Moore, in 1999.

Here are three impressions of racing that I painted in the early 1970s.

ABOVE: Ferrari at Monaco

UPPER RIGHT: Two Ferraris at Ontario

LOWER RIGHT: Denny Hulme in a McLaren

43/50   SAM POSEY '76

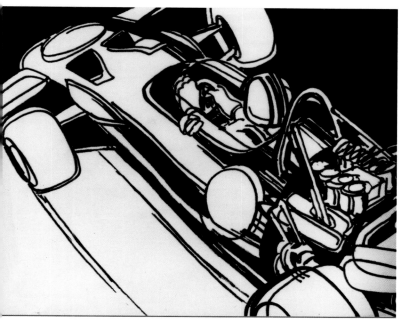

ABOVE: Lime Rock, 2013, with my daughter, Judy, and son, John, who is wearing one of my old driving suits.

RIGHT: Lime Rock Park owner Skip Barber stunned me with this tribute.

BELOW: A long, wonderful career ends the way it began, with laps at Lime Rock.

Von Trips was a German aristocrat whose home was his family's ancestral castle. He was a ladies' man and a risk-taker; his eleven-tenths driving had earned him the nickname Count von Crash. Ferrari's twin-nostril 156 had a 30 bhp advantage over the English cars, and Hill and von Trips traded wins and led the championship with ease. Unhappily for Phil, the vagaries of the season went the German's way, and at Monza, von Trips could clinch the championship with a third, even if Phil won.

Phil felt at home at Monza. The year before, it was where he'd had his first GP win, and in 1958 his first GP drive for Ferrari—flinging the car around and wearing a set of Engleberts down to the cords to convince Enzo that he could switch from sports cars (he won Le Mans three times) to the cut and thrust of F1.

Phil spoke Italian, and between races he lived in Modena, close to the Ferrari factory in Maranello. He loved music, and La Scala, the world-famous opera house, was nearby in Milan. In Italy, unlike the United States at the time, racing was regarded as a highly respectable profession, and Phil enjoyed the recognition that went along with being a Ferrari driver in Ferrari's hometown.

Partly to ensure victory and partly to rub salt in the wounds of the *Inglese*, Ferrari entered five cars at Monza. Von Trips grabbed the pole while Hill was fourth, almost a second back. Phil had been given the latest spec engine, but it felt flat. Ferrari himself tactlessly suggested the problem lay with Phil's right foot, but the engine was removed anyway, and later it was found to have a broken valve spring.

Race morning, Phil was up at six a.m. to check out the installation of the new motor, running the car on the infield roads and practicing starts. Later, he watched as von Trips, relaxed and funny, entertained a cluster of journalists. The German press was already hailing von Trips as the first German champion. To Phil, von Trips seemed too happy-go-lucky, yet at the same time the German's willingness to take risks could make Phil feel overly cautious. Of course, the count's risks didn't always pay off; at Monza alone, he had already crashed spectacularly—twice.

Thirty-two cars had qualified. Arranged two by two, they stretched along the straight for 300 yards. The race wasn't until three p.m., and the tension built steadily throughout the day, exacerbated by armed police patrolling the pits. The Ferraris were fitted with high axle ratios, and von Trips stumbled getting off the line and wound up at the back of a six-car pack. Jim Clark (Lotus), Graham Hill (BRM), and Jack Brabham.(Cooper) were in among the red cars, hoping to stay in their draft as long as they could. Phil got a perfect start, swept into the lead, and began to pull away.

On the second lap, he saw some wreckage near the edge of the track, but it was close to the braking zone for the next turn, and he barely glanced at it. A few laps later, he noticed von Trips was missing from his pit board, but that could mean anything. At one-third distance, the engines blew up in the Ferraris of both Ricardo Rodríguez and Giancarlo Baghetti. Phil eased off a little, and Richie Ginther, his close friend from the days when he had been Phil's riding mechanic in the Carrera Panamericana, brought his Ferrari into Phil's draft, signaling that he wasn't going to contest the lead. Dan Gurney was dueling with Stirling Moss for third. Ginther's engine failed at half distance, and soon afterward Moss dropped out, leaving Dan holding second, but well back. Six laps to go. Five. Phil's hastily fitted engine was the only Ferrari powerplant still running. One lap to go. Checkered flag.

He rolled to a stop, greeted by a somber reception. Von Trips was dead. He had touched wheels with Jim Clark, and both cars had veered out of control, the Ferrari scything into the crowd, killing 14. Phil was World Champion, and a giant laurel wreath was draped around his shoulders.

Much was made of whether or not he broke down sobbing. He did not. He had been at Le Mans in 1955 when 90 were killed, and by his count, 20 drivers had died in races that Phil himself had participated in. He had built emotional defenses, tricks that he used to convince himself that it couldn't happen to him.

But with typical introspection, he repeatedly reviewed racing's danger, and over time his view became, in effect, "It *can* happen to me, but because I love what I'm doing, and need to do it to feel whole, it's a risk I have to take." Racing drivers live in the moment; their highs and lows are acute but brief; the next race is always just ahead.

But von Trips had been killed at the end of the year, and Phil was a pallbearer at his funeral, slogging through the rain to the family chapel, a day when risk no longer seemed abstract.

People say that he backed into the championship. Not true. He and von Trips each had two wins, with Phil scoring more total points, 38 to 33. Each made one costly error—Hill's at Reims, where he spun while leading, von Trips's at Monza. The year's single best piece of driving was Phil's stunning pole lap at the Nürburgring, a track where he already held the lap record in sports cars. Overall, Phil had the speed, consistency, and mechanical savvy required of a great champion, and if you were to combine F1 with the World Sports Car Championship, which in those days attracted all the top GP drivers, Hill would have been the clear-cut winner.

At the end of the season, Ferrari's chief designer, Carlo Chiti, quit, along with the core management and design personnel of the F1 team. Nonetheless, 1962 started well for Phil, with a close second at Monaco and a pair of thirds. But as the year wore on, Chiti's absence—and the consequent lack of development—started to show. Phil was always at his best when he was doing something no one expected him to be able to do; now, with his car carrying the champion's No. 1, he was doing less.

After seven seasons with Ferrari, Phil signed on with Chiti and his fledgling team, ATS. But ATS lost their financial backing soon afterward, and Phil spent 1963 scraping around at the very back of the pack in a car that was ugly and looked unfinished. With each successive dismal performance the luster of his championship grew dimmer. He left ATS in 1964 and became a sort of journeyman driver, scratching for rides. One, for Cooper, summed things up: The car caught fire, and Phil, helpless to fight the flames, watched it burn to the ground. The descent from World Championship glory to this ignominy had taken only three years.

Outside of Formula One, however, being World Champion really meant something. He became a key player on Carroll Shelby's team of Cobras that would win the GT Championship, and he was Ford's Number One when they started their monumental effort to win Le Mans. Ultimately, though, Ford's corporate culture wasn't right for Phil, and when Jim Hall asked him to join Chaparral, he accepted.

Now began the final phase of his professional career. He admired Jim Hall, and it was good to drive a car that was on the cutting edge technically. Phil and Jo Bonnier won the Nürburgring 1000 Km with the Chaparral 2D—the first win in international competition for an automatic transmission. Later that summer, Phil won the Monterey Can-Am with Jim's radical, winged 2E. In 1967, Chaparral once again contested the classic endurance events, this time with the 2F, a winged coupe with distinctive slab sides.

The battle between Ford and Ferrari was at its zenith, and both companies were fielding four and five cars at every race. Hall had just one car, and Phil relished the team's underdog status. He led at Daytona, took the pole at Monza, and came from the back of the pack to lead at the Nürburgring—but the car suffered from gearbox failures, and it wasn't until Brands Hatch that it finished a race. It won, Phil sharing the drive with Mike Spence. It was to be Phil's last professional race. The phone continued to ring, but as Phil put it, "The offers just weren't the right ones." He was 39.

In retirement, he flourished. He indulged his love of music by adding to his collection of reproducing pianos, which re-create the exact touch of the pianist. I can remember sitting in his living room listening to a Rachmaninoff concerto recorded by Rachmaninoff himself. Phil was a perfectionist whose comprehensive understanding of anything mechanical made him one of the best car restorers in the business. His 1931 Pierce-Arrow won Best of Show at Pebble Beach, and his restoration business, Hill and Vaughn, attracted the most discerning collectors.

He was the expert commentator for ABC Sports when the network first covered racing, and Jim McKay, who knew top athletes all over the world, venerated Phil and delighted in imitating his distinctive way of speaking, the way he rushed his words together in little clumps—*Am-I-right-or-not?* Phil made no concessions to TV's compulsion to hype everything. For example, when the scoring monitors failed during the night at Le Mans, Jim tried manfully to reconstruct the running order. Then he turned to Phil, who said, live, "Let's face it, Jim—we have no idea what's going on."

He was uneasy making small talk, but he was well read, and welcomed a serious discussion on virtually any topic. He was a judge at Pebble Beach for 40 years. He was active in vintage racing, becoming almost as nervous as he had in his days as a pro. He teamed with John Lamm on a series of articles for this magazine describing what it was like to drive various historically significant (and priceless) racing cars—anything from a 1938 Mercedes-Benz W154 to Dale Earnhardt's Monte Carlo. These articles have been published in a wonderful book, *Phil Hill: A Driving Life,* and they reveal Phil at his best, showing his sense of humor, his acute powers of observation, and the sheer depth of his knowledge. He remained America's only champion for 16 years. It wasn't until 1978, a whole generation later, that Mario Andretti became the second American champion—in circumstances (at Monza, on the death of his teammate) eerily similar to Hill's.

Phil hadn't married when he was racing because he was unwilling to put someone he loved through the ordeal of being a driver's wife; but once he retired he startled his friends by marrying Alma, a bighearted extrovert. They had two daughters and a son, Derek, a talented driver in his own right. The Hills lived comfortably in Santa Monica, in the house Phil grew up in, surrounded by his trophies, the special pianos, and a couple of spectacular Packards in the garage. Dan Gurney, Phil's friend since the days when they were both new to F1, lived just an hour away, and they stayed close. Even heroes have heroes, and Dan was on top of Phil's list.

I last saw Phil at his 80th birthday, a glittering evening in Jay Leno's garage, attended by over 1,000 people eager to wish him well. He was fighting a particularly virulent form of Parkinson's disease and had a little over a year to live. He could barely speak, but he nevertheless insisted on questioning me about a fine point of the current F1 scene.

Phil was a survivor in racing's most dangerous era, something in which he took quiet pride, along with the championship he won that remarkable day at Monza. Today, we look back and savor Phil's achievement—as one might savor a Rachmaninoff concerto, say, or a finely restored Pierce-Arrow . . . or a man like no other.

The great opera house La Scala is just down the road, and every year I ask my editor for some Pavarotti, but so far, no luck.

Most of my teases start by establishing where we are and something about the atmosphere. If I can get this done quickly I'll have room for an extra sentence later on. Just as the Iditarod is about the cold, Monza is about Ferrari—and every fan makes that connection instantly. It gives me a wonderful head start. Equally obvious is that Ferraris are red, so there should be a lot of red in the piece.

Monza '11

There is no team like Ferrari, and for Ferrari there is no track like Monza: flat and fast—home ground, the factory just down the road. Fernando Alonso, Felipe Massa—not just drivers today, but inheritors of a glory-filled tradition, men on a mission inviolate—doing battle for the honor of a nation—today, at this track.

But this year Sebastian Vettel is at home on every track,

a place reserved for him at the front of every grid,

the most difficult turns his comfort zone. Anyone ahead of him is trespassing in his house.

Jenson Button, Lewis Hamilton, Mark Webber; they have managed to look inside, but only briefly.

Ferrari won here last year, Vettel three years ago . . . who can call Monza home today? Who holds the keys?

The time to find out is now.

The Grand Prix of Italy, at Monza, is . . . *next!*

Monza '14

Ask any team boss who he or she would most like to have driving for them, and the answer will be the same— Fernando Alonso.

When he signed with Ferrari in 2010, Alonso had already won two World Championships, and looked a sure bet to win many more. But it hasn't happened. Ferrari—with the biggest budget in racing—has a technical department that's in shambles and cannot build the car Alonso deserves.

The team is squandering the talent of a man who can make passes where passes can't be made (Silverstone, passing Vettel into a copse), who race after race carries the car on his back (Austria), and who can force a midfield car to the front (Spa). And he's just plain fast, consistently outrunning his teammate, Kimi Raikkonen.

Today, racing on Ferrari's home track, in front of the highly critical Italian press and fans starved for success, the team needs Alonso like they've never needed him before. A podium would save face; a win would save the season. To achieve either would take a miracle—but then miracles are Alonso's business.

Dan and his wife Evi are two of the nicest people I know. As I write this, they are preparing an immense tome that will cover virtually every detail of Dan's illustrious career. Buy it.

Introduction for Road Racing Drivers Club Honoree: Dan Gurney

LONG BEACH, CALIFORNIA, APRIL 16, 2009

When he was a boy, Dan Gurney saw a tomato plant that had grown up through asphalt and, against all odds, blossomed. It could be the story of Dan's career; as a driver, a car builder, and a car owner, he has never had it easy, yet he has always found a way to win.

He brought Porsche and Brabham their first championship wins. He won Le Mans for Ford with A. J. Foyt, and he won in USAC, NASCAR, and the Can-Am. He built cars that won Indy—five times—and in the last few months, he built the revolutionary Delta Wing and ran it at Le Mans. He broke into Formula One in 1959 when it was at its most dangerous; his team, Ferrari, had lost both their lead drivers; a seat was open, Dan took it, and finished second in his second GP, on the deadly high banks of Avus. He left Ferrari because he disliked the politics; over the next six years he established a reputation as one of the best in the business; in fact, the great Jim Clark said Dan was the only driver he really feared. Dan was a hired gun, but he had a keen interest in the way cars were designed and built. In the mid-1960s Goodyear was just getting into racing, and to win they had to beat Firestone. They suffered an acute embarrassment in 1964 at Indy when, on the eve of the race, Goodyear-shod cars switched to Firestones.

Goodyear was looking for teams that would be loyal to their brand, and Carroll Shelby brokered a deal that made him partners with Dan in a Goodyear-backed team. Its primary target was Indy, but F1 rules were nearly identical, and Dan was able to negotiate the financing for an F1 team as well.

The tomato plant was about to thrust through the asphalt.

The track at Spa lies in a region that was a particularly bloody battleground during World War II, and when I write about the dangers facing any driver here, I am mindful that this is sport, not war, and any risk a driver takes is voluntary—one he can back away from—whereas for the soldier, there was no way out.

Monaco has its harbor, Spa has the Ardennes forest—physical features that by themselves go a long way toward establishing a mood. Dark forests are scary—wolves and witches live there—and when you add swirling mists and the very fast section known as Eau Rouge, you have ingredients that would inspire Wagner.

Spa '08

The forest of the Ardennes, dense with pines and history. The track here diving through deep descending valleys, soaring like a great bird catching a mountain updraft, twisting through the forest stronghold, its broad asphalt swath bringing, each year, the new cars to this ancient place called Spa.

It is here, racing on public roads, that Formula One digs back to its roots. It is here that the great masters of Spa—Jim Clark, Ayrton Senna, Michael Schumacher—have used the danger and difficulty of the track to leave lesser men far behind. And it is here that two Americans, Dan Gurney and the late Phil Hill, scored stirring victories.

Today the focus is on Kimi Raikkonen. He has won three GPs in a row here, and now he must win a fourth—not to earn a spot in the pantheon of great Spa drivers (he's already done that), but to save his season and his standing within the Ferrari team. He is the defending World Champion, but he hasn't been driving like it, or acting like it, either, and his status as Ferrari's number one is shaky at best.

But Spa can change all that. Sure, there aren't any more championship points to be won here than at other races, but a victory today could turn skeptics into believers, and make it difficult for Ferrari to designate

Felipe Massa as team leader. Who will Ferrari choose to attack Lewis Hamilton? At the end of the day today, we should know.

Spa is the crucible, its dark forests an impartial witness to the doings of men. And what will they see today? Find out, as you watch. The Grand Prix of Belgium at Spa is . . . *next!*

Spa '11

Danger haunts its history, apprehension swirls like the mists of the Ardennes.

The fastest turns in F1 are here, slicing through the forest, soaring up the valley walls . . . each car a brief glimpse of color, a machine with a pounding pulse, invisible molecular constructions, straining, building speed.

This is Spa, where a driver's mask of confidence fools no one. Collisions on the first lap . . . slippery roads . . . electrifying finishes. A race-long hazard zone.

The longest lap in F1, an always unpredictable race—yet the multiple winners are the great drivers of the sport.

(Graphics: Schumacher 6 wins, Senna 5 wins, Clark 4 wins, Fangio 3 wins)

Racing here is racing on the edge; the essence of F1—and it's just moments away.

The Grand Prix of Belgium, at Spa is . . . *next!*

Introduction for Road Racing Drivers Club Honoree: Roger Penske

LONG BEACH, CALIFORNIA, APRIL 14, 2011

I n American racing in the late 1960s there was something in the air, something not yet defined. It wasn't concealed; it was right out there for anyone to see—anyone, that is, with an eye for the kind of change that comes at you slowly, and yet leaves no doubt that the change is profound, and there will be no turning back.

First we noticed "The Look," the midnight blue cars so quietly elegant that all of the other cars seemed shabby by comparison. Next came the winning—the blue cars dominating race after race. Finally it was Roger Penske himself, whose ambition, focus, and relentless hard work drove the team, putting success out of reach for anyone unwilling to make his sacrifices and match his commitment. Right there at Penske Racing was the dawn of the professionalism we now take for granted.

And Roger kept raising his game, year after year, and in series after series. The USRRC (while it lasted) and the Trans-Am were like private game preserves. In the Can-Am, the McLarens were a tough nut to crack, so in partnership with Porsche he created a sledgehammer—the Porsche 917/30, quite possibly the car more superior to its opposition than any in racing history. Conclusive proof of the team's ability came when they won Indy and it seemed like business as usual.

He had you beat from boardroom to pit wall. Wearing his perfectly polished Guccis, he ran his show, hands-on, meticulous, listening to what his men had to say, loyal, brilliant at choosing the right people for the job. He was always available, driving his men hard and himself even harder. He could outthink you, outspend you; he had better connections than you did, grander plans. And he never looked back.

Roger is 77, and still runs winning teams. He has made vast amounts of money, and he did it the old-fashioned way: building things, being loyal to his employees, gambling big when opportunities arose. I drove a Trans-Am Camaro for him in the summer of 1968, and just before the start he'd lean in the window and tell me, "Don't go berserk, and don't get involved." Good advice.

He had been a world-class driver who retired early to launch his career in business. The team's first full-time driver was Mark Donohue, who was to other drivers what Roger was to other team owners. Mark was very, very hard to beat, and his dedication to the team matched Roger's. By the time of Mark's tragic death, the standards had been set, the bar raised high for those who followed, for Rick Mears and Bobby Unser, for Mario Andretti, Danny Sullivan, Hélio Castroneves, and Will Power. To sit in a Penske cockpit was racing's highest honor, and those who did knew what was expected.

Roger's business life has a limitless trajectory. He controls more than 300 car dealerships, a giant truck-leasing enterprise he bought from Hertz, factories manufacturing diesel engines, truck parts, and electrical systems—and much more.

Roger has always looked at numbers to tell the story, and today, his figures—over 36,000 employees, a net worth of more than two billion dollars—would seem phenomenal if it weren't for an exponential growth rate that will soon make today's holdings seem meager.

Those of us who were lucky enough to have known him when he was just starting out could see he was going to be successful, but not even in moments of the most extravagant optimism would any of us have predicted that Roger would rise so far. Like many success stories, hard work and ambition form the core. But with Roger the foundation was laid in meeting the highly specific demands of racing. So as we honor him tonight, we can truly say, "He is one of us."

In 1974 Jackie Stewart was ABC's "color commentator" (that was the term) for racing. He was newly retired, and his three World Championships put him in a class with Indy stars A. J. Foyt and Mario Andretti, the biggest names in Indy car racing. ABC was lucky to have him.

That year, the 500 was the day after Monaco, and, with the Concorde as the centerpiece of his plan, Jackie intended to be in the booth for both races. It would be tight, but Jackie was no stranger to close connections. Then somebody at ABC took a look at the schedule and got cold feet—it was too big a risk to go into Indy—one of the highest-rated shows of the year—without a color man. So they gave Jackie the choice: Indy or Monaco—and he picked Monaco.

Now the network was looking for someone to take his place, and the next thing I knew, I was in the ABC booth, about to try my hand at being a color commentator. The track goes green—practice. Out comes Tom Sneva. Jim McKay nods to me. I ID Sneva and say a couple of things about him. Then, figuring less is more, I shut up. Later, in the sacred ground of the ABC compound, everyone is pleased. I've passed the test, and I've got a job. It will last 22 years.

Glimpses from the Booth

ROAD & TRACK, SEPTEMBER 1991

Tuesday, May 7

I check in at the Speedway Motel on the grounds of the track, just behind the turn two grandstands. I am assigned the same room year after year, and I open the door to find everything exactly as I left it last May. This is my 17th year as a commentator with ABC Television, and my 25th Indy.

From my window I see an attendant filling the pool with a hose, and in the distance golfers are intent upon their games, the urgent business of the track going unnoticed. I hear the whine of a car going through turn two, then fading away down the backstretch. A few seconds later, the sound of the engine is back: Another lap of Indy is complete. Everyday stuff here in May.

In a sense, every lap is the same: four left turns, two and a half miles. And yet no two laps are ever *driven* exactly the same way. I switch on the Speedway's special closed-circuit TV and watch the car heading again down the backstretch, lighter now by eight pounds of fuel than the last lap, the tires worn a fraction more. Now as the car swings to the wall to begin its trajectory across the north end of the track, the sun breaks through, instantly warming the asphalt and the air. I see the light sparkle on the car and know that the driver cocooned inside is changing his line, if only by a fraction.

At no track in the world is perfection approached so closely, only because drivers do more laps here than anywhere else. At times this perfection can breed the notion that nothing can go wrong, that danger is held in check by skill and knowledge, that the high wire has an invisible net.

On my spare bed, I arrange the folders containing my notes. On race day, Paul Page will do the play-by-play, Bobby Unser will deal with strategy and technical information, while my assignment is to give you a feeling for the personalities of the drivers.

My thickest folder is labeled A. J. FOYT. A. J. has announced that this will be his last Indy, and I am working with ABC's Emilie Deutsch on a Foyt "piece" for the pre-race show.

Wednesday, May 8
Emilie and I go to the Speedway Museum to see the four cars that Foyt drove to victory here. Looking very dated, they are grouped in a sort of shrine. We overhear a small boy ask his dad, "Is A. J. Foyt dead?" The reality of A. J. is that the accomplishments that make him a legend are buried in history, but I can't write the piece purely as history,

Pit interviews at Indy. I was more comfortable in the booth.

because A. J. is still very much alive and will be in the race. The duality of Foyt past and present; the piece must capture that.

The ABC compound is located in the shadow of the stands behind the pits. Visitors fresh from admiring the cars in Gasoline Alley are surprised by the scale of our operation (150 people, including 90 engineers, work this show) but disappointed in the aesthetics. The high-tech hardware of television is crammed into a very low-tech collection of trailers, tents, trucks, and temporary plywood structures. Wires run everywhere, but study a diagram and you'll see that most of them wind up in the main control room, referred to, simply, as "the truck." This is the nerve center of our operation, and it is here, on race day, where producer Bob Goodrich and director Don Ohlmeyer will make the decisions that create our show.

It is one of the enduring ironies of television that the better Goodrich and Ohlmeyer do their jobs, the easier people at home think television is. For example, this year we have 42 cameras, and because they are positioned everywhere from the Goodyear blimp to on board Rick Mears's car, the expectation is created that we can see, and hear, everything.

But unlike, say, football or baseball, where 90 percent of the action is focused around the ball, in racing the story may break out anywhere. Suppose you are Don Ohlmeyer sitting in the control room, confronted by 42 monitors. How do you keep track? Which shot do you use? Ordinary coverage of one lap by one car calls into play roughly seven cameras. If you used the same shots in the same sequence for the next lap, the show would look stale. So Don will shake things up, changing the shots and the timing, to create a metaphor for the speed of the race.

Other elements include graphics and music. In addition, we will have pre-taped pieces, such as the Foyt piece, plus "sound bites" from driver interviews, historical footage, and track facts—a grab bag of more than 100 items, each timed to the second. Goodrich and Ohlmeyer must use this arsenal to develop whatever story is emerging during the race.

Sometimes the choices are tough: Is a report from the pits better than track action? Does a shot of Sandy Andretti cheering for Michael tell you more about Michael than watching him drive? There will be 3,000 camera cuts during the race, not one of which will be made with the luxury of time.

Last year, on the evening before the race, I came across Don sitting on the steps of a trailer, his head buried in his hands as he tried to visualize the start and imagine in what sequence he would cut his cameras. You can prepare, but you can never, truly, be ready. The Indy 500 has never been the same twice.

Friday, May 10

The day before qualifying, the track has been open for six days (and more than 7,000 laps have been recorded), yet so far no driver has crashed or even spun. It is hot, and the air is charged with tension. When the first incident finally occurs, just after lunch, it is spooky that the driver crashing into the turn one wall should be Rick Mears, because Rick has *never* crashed, or even spun, in 14 years of racing and testing at Indianapolis. It is a symmetry contrived by the dark gods of the Speedway, and there is more to come.

5:09 p.m. Rick, taken downtown to Methodist Hospital for a checkup, has returned to drive his backup car. He has just ripped off a lap as fast as his previous best in his old car. Because the mechanical failure that caused his crash has yet to be diagnosed, his run exhibits more than just skill—it is an act of faith and courage, and his crew, rarely demonstrative, gives him a standing ovation.

I am in the announcers' booth, rehearsing for tomorrow's broadcast of qualifying, and on the monitor, toward the bottom of the screen, I see Rick rolling in and the upraised arms of his Penske crew—the exact instant the top of the shot erupts in chaos, a car crashing into the end of the pit wall, people running. Mark Dismore, a 31-year-old rookie, is severely injured, and by the end of the day we learn that he will face months of recuperation.

Triumph and disaster, on the screen, at the same time.

Saturday, May 11

The day belongs to A. J. Foyt, who, at the age of 56, qualifies for the front row of his 34th consecutive Indy 500. We are on the air with a three-hour qualifying show, and A. J., first in line, leads it off.

Goodrich and Ohlmeyer orchestrate a sequence that begins with A. J.'s engine being started (a close-up, from under the rear wing) and Chief Steward Tom Binford's final instructions (Binford is wired for sound), then switches to multiple-camera coverage as A. J. pulls out through a mass of photographers to begin his run. For once there is no question of where to focus or what the story is. The driver with the mythic past is about to perform in the present.

His run is excellent, but as Jack Arute interviews him, tears well in A. J.'s eyes. It is strong TV, and a showcase for Jack's interviewing skills, but it is agony to see how bittersweet this moment is for A. J. To him, his last Indy is like putting one foot in the grave. He planned to retire at the end of this year; now you see him not so sure.

Rick Mears gets the pole—his sixth, a record. Business as usual, until you remember that the car he meant to drive sits wrecked back in the garage.

Thursday, May 23

Carburetion day. The cars are on the track for the last time before the race. Paul, Bobby, and I are in the announcers' booth for a dry run. The booth is on the roof of the main grandstands, five stories above the main straight, and the view of the pits, the infield, and the Indianapolis skyline is the best. But we rarely look out the windows; we look at the monitors.

Paul stands in the middle, with Bobby to his right and me on the left. In addition to two program monitors off which we call the race, we also have scoring monitors and "net return"—our show as it is actually appearing on the air, delayed four seconds by its 22,000-mile round-trip through space to the satellite. To my left is a "Telestrator," which enables me to draw diagrams in the manner of John Madden.

We wear headsets with microphones. In one ear we hear our voices, the sounds of the track, and music. In the other, we hear instructions from the truck—for example, "Ten seconds to commercial," "Lead to Punch with Doctor Boch," or "20 seconds to Luyendyk sound bite number six." Most of this is for Paul, who is skilled at maintaining a smooth flow of commentary even as people are shouting in his ear. It is Paul's job, also, to orchestrate comments from Bobby and me, taking into account not only the content of what we might say, but also the style.

Bobby and I work together well, I believe, because we are opposites—the "Odd Couple," we have been called. For years I was ABC's only analyst in the booth, and my romanticized, somewhat abstract view of racing omitted the gritty, down-to-earth quality that is also part of the sport, and which Bobby now brings to our telecast. We sometimes disagree, which only proves that two people who are experienced in racing and who care passionately about it can see the same thing differently. When the action is dull on the race track, a sharp exchange in the booth can be entertaining, and entertainment is part of our job.

Plus, Bobby is occasionally right.

Saturday, May 25

The night before the race. In my room, the spare bed, once piled with papers, is cleared; everything I'll take to the booth tomorrow is copied into just two notebooks. The phone, which for days has rung constantly, is silent, the message light off. Outside, the pool, full now and brightly lit, is a shimmering turquoise.

Sunday, May 26

Race day. I pull back the curtains. In the half-light of dawn, the pool is gray and dimpled with rain. At the compound, Goodrich and Ohlmeyer know that our carefully rehearsed pre-race show will have to be expanded—but by how much? Swiftly, they format additional segments.

The rain stops at 8:30 a.m., and as our show begins at 10:00, the track is drying. For an hour, we air the new segments, composed chiefly of pieces from what Bob Goodrich calls our "saddlebags," and interviews by our pit reporters, Jack Arute, Gary Gerould, and Dr. Jerry Punch. Willy T. Ribbs, the first African American ever to make the race, is gracious and confident. Emerson Fittipaldi is flat on his back in the Penske garages, doing leg exercises. Gary Bettenhausen, the star-crossed driver whose father was killed here 30 years ago, looks composed for a man who might have his best chance to win in years.

Just after 11:00, Chief Steward Binford tells us the start is now 45 minutes away, and we segue into our pre-planned format. The Foyt piece airs, a touch of *film noir*, with me telling my son John about the legend of A. J., as John and I walk through turn one at twilight. Minutes later comes my appearance on camera. Being on TV produces a heightened awareness of yourself—how you look, how you speak, who you are. Anyone who has been in a home video has experienced these sensations, but you feel extra layers of intensity when the eye of a network camera is upon you. I describe the historic front row of Mears, Foyt, and Andretti as a "sort of Mount Rushmore of racing."

Down on the track, the ceremonies for this 75th running of the 500 are in full swing. It is a goal of our pre-race show to make you feel as if you are at the event, but for me the tension of the start (now just minutes away), coupled with the emotions of "Taps" and "Back Home Again in Indiana," is too much. I remove my headset and try to distract myself with a last look at my notes. We have been on the air for two hours.

At the start, a quick view from Michael Andretti's cockpit in the second row is followed by a wide shot, showing the huge crowd, the camera pushing in as the front row crosses the famous yard of bricks. Two hundred laps to go. Now we're with Duane Sweeney as he waves the flags, now on a wide shot of turn one, Mears leading, Mario close behind, now to the short chute, Foyt fading. But something is wrong in turn one, and the yellow caution lights have flashed on around the track.

Ohlmeyer stays on the leaders, buying time while our tape operators scan the machines (23 of them), which continuously record certain designated cameras. Soon the replays are ready and we see what triggered the incident: Gary Bettenhausen, fighting a huge slide along the apron. The second replay from a higher angle shows the consequences: rookie Buddy Lazier into the outside wall, the nose of his car damaged. Now we see the first angle again, this time in slow motion.

Under the green, Rick Mears begins to drop back. Mario Andretti leads, then Michael. My notes arrayed in front of me, I look for windows of opportunity to dart in with a line or two about the driver we see on the screen, or to connect a researched fact with the current action. Sometimes I have a good line ready just as we shift to another car, and I have to change plans in mid-sentence. Awkward, but as Emerson Fittipaldi put it about driving: "Always think ahead of you, never behind."

Lap 24: Kevin Cogan and Roberto Guerrero are in the wall of turn four. Debris has damaged Foyt's car, and as he drives slowly to the pits, A. J.'s wave to the crowd has the look of an emotional farewell. Producer's choice: Do you concentrate on Cogan being cut out of his car, or on Foyt in what might be the final moments of his legendary career at Indy? Goodrich sticks with Foyt.

At half distance, Michael Andretti has been leading so long that most of my Michael notes have scribbles through them. On lap 104, with Michael still leading, we see Mears, running fifth, in the same frame: Is Michael about to put him a lap down? Later, Rick will tell me, "I was a little nervous, but I was watching him, and the rate of closure had slowed. We had something left in the pocket." Michael has cut a tire; his stop for a replacement on lap 109 gets Rick off the hook and puts Emerson Fittipaldi into the lead.

Fittipaldi! Now I have pages of fresh notes, and my Penske material can resurface. Emerson has been patient, working his way through the pack from his 15th starting spot; now he leads the 500 for the third time in three years. As Paul recaps the standings, Michael is 2nd, Bobby Rahal 3rd. USAC's electronic scoring has failed, and thus our own system, downstream of USAC's, is inoperable, but our scorers in the booth, working by hand, are keeping us in the game. Spotters around the track inform the truck of the battles back in the pack, and Don occasionally switches to these, but the action is all up front.

At three-quarter distance, Fittipaldi has Michael Andretti filling his mirrors, and Mears is catching them both. With 33 laps to go, it is a three-car race, but suddenly Jack Arute reports that Fittipaldi has a clutch problem. Quickly, the pit announcers and their cameramen move into position, and when Emerson pits, we are ready with four-camera coverage. But this time it isn't what we see that tells the story—it is what we hear. Emerson, frantically trying to dump the car into gear as he's pushed out, strips the gears. Now it is a two-car race, and we have cameras in both.

After a yellow, during which Michael pits for fuel, the green flag waves with 15 laps to go. The moment for what Rick Mears will call "the shoot-out" is at hand. We are on board with Michael, looking up the track at the cars he must pass to get to Rick. We ride with Michael as he feints left, now right, heads into turn one outside of Rick, and executes a remarkable outside pass. You want to savor this, but now Rick is coming down the front straight, ready to counterattack.

"The only lane open," he will tell me after the race, "was the high groove. Talk about the unknown—I'd never run that high. The key was that, thanks to the slow laps under yellow, my tires were cool. I knew that if I could get through the turbulence [behind Michael's car] and get alongside him, I'd get clean air again."

Pass! Wide shot of the crowd. Split screen: Chris Mears, jubilant, her fists thrust into the air; Sandy Andretti, tense. Twelve laps to go. On board again with Michael—Rick is stretching his lead.

Like everyone else, I am thrilled by the brilliance of these two drivers and excited by the sudden turn of events. But it is my job to concentrate on what is going on, and to put in perspective what a fourth Mears Indy win would mean. I talk about it first from his point of view, then about the dynamic equilibrium of a race that began focused on four-time winner Foyt and is ending with the crowning of a new four-time winner. Live television: Those of us who produce it share in the experience of what we cover—not after the fact, but as it is happening.

After a last yellow bunches the much-depleted field, Mears has an empty track ahead as the green flag waves. We are aboard his car, we see exactly what he sees exactly as he sees it: the Indianapolis Speedway, each lap two and a half miles long, with four left turns, the same as always, but changed somehow, because he is driving it now to his fourth, and finest, victory.

Tom Bryant and I wanted to do an article about the CART vs. IRL wars. It was a subject that had been beaten to death, and we were looking for a fresh angle. We settled on what it would be like to check in at the Speedway Motel and find that Mario, A. J., Al, Bobby—all the drivers that were the living legends of the 500—weren't there. Was Indy really Indy without them? What counted most, the drivers or the track?

The race would go on, of course, but the connection with an era that stretched back to the end of World War II was severed.

CART and the IRL would be reconciled, but the motel, built in 1963, would be torn down in 2009. I had spent 20 Mays there, and when I went to Indy recently, it was a shock to find it gone, without a trace.

Where Everyone Knows Your Name

ROAD & TRACK, SEPTEMBER 1997

When you drive east along 16th Street in Speedway, Indiana, home of the Indianapolis 500, and look left, your attention fixed on the back of the track's looming grandstands, it is easy to miss the motel that sits just outside of turn two. Unless it happens to be your home, which is how I have felt about the place for almost 20 years. My home in May.

It is not much to look at: just two stories with a flat roof, steel-reinforced concrete, picture windows, small white bricks—a style that said "modern" in the 1950s, but seems meager in these more hedonistic times. Ninety-six rooms are arranged in three blocks, connected by breezeways. Outside stairs and walkways; no hallways or elevators. Lots of asphalt and, except for race day, always a place to park.

Until this year, it was called the Speedway Motel, but the changing world at Indy (the additions of the NASCAR race and the championship golf course, plus the unhappy CART vs. IRL standoff) has affected the motel too. I stayed there for a couple of days the week of this year's 500 and was startled to find that it has been renamed; it is now the Brickyard Crossing Motel and Resort. The wonderfully tacky sign with its cluster of flags and the space for messages ("Congratulations, Mario!") is gone, and the doors and trim have been repainted; instead of pavement gray, they are now fairway green.

And, of course, Mario is nowhere to be found. Or Michael, or Rick, or Little Al. The absence of these great champions is profoundly disturbing: They, along with many others who stayed here, made much of the history that is Indy, and without them the place feels empty, as if the reality of the motel resided in those people, and not in its bricks and concrete. Years of continuity have been severed, and drivers and car owners who dedicated their lives to Indy have discovered that Indy is quite prepared to go on without them. (I understood this in the abstract before my visit—understood that I would not be seeing many familiar faces. The shock was seeing the new faces. They have moved right in, eager to make their own history.)

Building the motel was part of the rejuvenation of the Speedway undertaken by Tony Hulman after World War II. The wealthy, patrician Mr. Hulman may have had in mind the fishing camps or hunting lodges he so enjoyed, a place for his friends to stay when they came for his race. "When d'ja get in?" was Mr. Hulman's famous greeting, and he was truly welcoming you as a guest. The motel was his guesthouse, a place where other gentlemen of means, possessed of sporting instincts, could meet one another and a handful of the drivers in an atmosphere consistent with the business at hand.

Of course there had to be a bar, a place where the deeds of the day could be discussed and properly embellished. Handsomely paneled, it is enlivened with some of LeRoy Neiman's early paintings—fine, impressionistic views of the track in the 1960s when roadsters held sway. Racing cars are visible in the lobby, too, and these are real ones, brought over from the collection of the Speedway Museum. The restaurant has a checkered-flag motif, and if you order waffles at breakfast, they will arrive embossed with the silhouette of an early rear-engine car, perhaps a Huffaker. Although a waiting list has long existed for rooms in May, this is not a private club; Mr. Hulman was too egalitarian—and too shrewd a businessman—for that. Anyone can walk right into the bar or restaurant and, with a little luck, be seated at a table next to A. J. Foyt.

Until the recent spate of condo/skyboxes at NASCAR tracks, only a very few circuits offered a place to stay right on the grounds—most notably the Nürburgring in Germany, where the SportHotel is across from the pits. Staying at either place offers a rare chance for total immersion in racing, but at the Speedway—oops, Brickyard Crossing—it is not for just a weekend; it is for a month. Most guests coming for the 500 arrive in the chill of mid-spring and do not leave until the first heat of approaching summer. For me, checking in meant checking out of the rest of my life.

Once in, time exists only as a countdown to the race. And time gets distorted; as the days that remain grow fewer, they increase in intensity. Three days from the race, it feels just as far off as it did three weeks before. It is the same for all; motel guests share emotions like passengers on a ship.

For many years, when I covered the 500 for ABC TV and was a regular, Griff at reservations always saved me the same room, just as she would for Bobby or Danny or Roger. My room (I will always think of it that way, even if I discover Dale Earnhardt in there, or—worse—some linksman) is on the upper floor, facing the track. In the foreground of the view is the motel's pool, rarely used, but occasionally a driver's wife or girlfriend will decide to work on her tan, and it is always a curious sight to see a bikini out there amid the sea of cars. The golf course, splendidly green, is across the parking lot to the right, and the back of the turn two grandstand is to the left, just 75 yards away—so close that when Rick Mears hit the wall there in 1991, the concussive blast rocked the motel.

Indeed, for good or bad, when you stay at the motel, you cannot escape the track. In the morning, when the cars begin to warm up, it is as if a large animal has awakened with a low growl. When they are up to speed, the animal seems to be rapidly inhaling and exhaling, perhaps in pursuit of something. Before the rules changed for this year, the sound of a car racing away down the backstretch toward turn three was excruciatingly beautiful, a whine that seemed to soar from octave to higher octave before passing out of the range of hearing . . . 245 mph, maybe more, the sound, perhaps, of a new track record, of history being made. This year, with a field of stock blocks, it was more like trucks droning by on an interstate. But either way, the sound is reassuring.

It is the sudden silence that scares you. Has someone crashed? The rooms have closed-circuit TV, with continuous coverage from the track, so you quickly turn your set on, and are relieved to see that this time it is just a tow-in.

But the danger is never truly out of your mind. Too often, a room has suddenly been freed up because its occupant is moving down 16th Street to Methodist Hospital. After a bad crash, everyone knows, and even the room-service waiter will talk in hushed tones. During the replays on the evening news, you sense that every TV set in the place is on; you feel a kind of collective tension, as if the walls didn't exist.

Perhaps because of this emotional intimacy, guests go out of their way not to intrude on one another's social lives. Your door left ajar does not invite visitors; drivers who meet by chance on the stairs may pass with only a nod without seeming rude. And the switchboard is a real ally. One year, I was being inundated by calls the night before the race (it was my birthday), and a motherly operator cut in to ask if I hadn't better be getting to sleep. End of calls.

Every room, I suspect, can tell its own story. On the second floor, there is the room in which Robert Wagner seduced Paul Newman's wife, Joanne Woodward. Of course, this was fiction—it happened in the movie *Winning* (Newman delights in pointing out the room to friends)—but life has often imitated art in this motel. A favorite memory of mine was going to see Jackie Stewart just after he had arrived from Europe one year. When the door opened and I peered into the dark, there was the wee Scotsman, in his boxers, surrounded by 100 cases of champagne—a bizarre sight, until Jackie explained that he was representing Moët; the cases were to be delivered to the VIP suites.

Each year, the last days before the race—starting with the so-called Carburetion Day on Thursday—combine the languor of early summer with the frenzy of last-minute preparations. A stack of plastic glasses (decorated with the logo of the race) appears on the vanity as a sort of sanction (*Let the party begin!*), and the message light, winking red, signals that the special race-day parking passes can be picked up at the front desk. Already traffic is choking 16th Street, a long line stretches down the hall from the restaurant, and fans can be seen milling in the parking lot.

By the eve of the race, the place is under siege. Bombs and fireworks are going off in the field across the street. College kids are diving fully clothed into the pool. Searchlights have been set up on the fairways, and their beams crisscross the night sky. Someone pounds on your door, then on the next one, and the next. You wonder how you will get to sleep—on this night of all nights, when sleep is so important.

The sweaty hours drag by, and the wake-up call at 5:30 a.m. is actually a welcome relief. A quick look outside to check the weather; if it is clear, you know that the waiting is almost over, and that the countdown now is no longer in days; it is in hours. Dan Gurney once said that when you brush your teeth on the morning of the Indy 500, you wonder if you will ever be brushing them again. I drove in the race only once, but I know

Dan was right. As I dress, I think of the drivers in the motel who will soon be getting up and brushing their teeth. Then it is time to leave, to walk to the pits.

After the race, I will be back to grab my bags before the dash to the airport. By then, the motel will be nearly empty, doors left open, trash blowing in the wind. It is always a strange moment—leaving home to go home.

Most of my fan mail comes from fans who are collecting autographs of all living Indy and Formula One drivers. Typically a letter will include a photograph for me to sign, and return postage. A great many come from the Baltic countries, and you can feel the effort as the writer struggles with English.

The rest of the mail falls in the miscellaneous category, which is dominated by the 1970 Trans-Am. I was in the thick of it, driving a lime-green Dodge Challenger, which is still being raced today. This article tells the story of that famous summer from my point of view.

Trans-Am Memories
HAGERTY CLASSIC CARS, FEBRUARY 2012

You went to a Trans-Am race and saw cars that closely resembled the one you drove there, only with racing numbers: This was the concept. It was also the myth.

Almost nothing but the body—and more on that later—remained from the original cars. Non-stock components included massive brakes, wide racing wheels and tires, special transmissions and differentials, adjustable shocks, revised suspension geometry, and high-revving 305 CID V8s that put out over 450hp. The roll cage was there ostensibly for safety, but really as a space frame designed to stiffen the chassis.

I raced in the Trans-Am from 1968 to 1970, three years during which its popularity and significance grew exponentially. In 1968, I drove a

Camaro for Roger Penske's championship team as a backup, in case one of the Ford guys took out the team's star, Mark Donohue. In 1969, driving a Shelby Mustang, I won the only race I entered, which turned out to be Carroll's last pro win. In hindsight, however, all the excitement and intrigue of the races of the late 1960s, so important to me at the time, would come to be seen merely as curtain raisers for the grand opera of 1970. In 1970 GM, Ford, Chrysler, and American Motors all descended on the Trans-Am as if winning it was the Holy Grail, a surefire way to

I wrote this article for a magazine published by the Hagerty Insurance people. A great assignment, allowing me to relive the 1970 season.

enlarge their share of the lucrative pony-car market. Chevrolet was the defending champion, but Penske had surprised everyone by forsaking GM and making a rumored $5 million deal with American Motors to run their Javelin. Chevy turned to Jim Hall, and he prepared for battle under the Chaparral banner. Pontiac signed 1967 Trans-Am champ Jerry Titus. In earlier years, Ford had gone with two teams, but they didn't renew Shelby, and concentrated their budget on NASCAR veteran Bud Moore. Chrysler's original plan was also for just one team—Dan Gurney's All American Racers (AAR)—preparing a Plymouth Barracuda for Dan's promising protégé, Swede Savage. But the Dodge division lobbied successfully for a slice of the action for their Challenger, and I got to drive it, for Ray Caldwell's Autodynamics team. Add a dozen top-notch privateers, and you had an entry list that read like a who's who of its day.

A stock pony car was priced within reach of young men and women buying their first car. The advertising strategies all focused on a sporty image, and one after another, the manufacturers decided to go racing. The trouble was that second place was useless to the ad boys, and the strength of the entry list made winning as difficult as it was significant. Week after week Dodge readied their full-page ads ("Posey Drives Challenger to Trans-Am Win") but never got to use any of them. Except for a lone win by Chaparral, Penske and Bud Moore swept the boards.

All of us who were driving for factory teams also raced in other series—Indy, Can-Am, F5000—in which the cars were far faster. We called the Trans-Am cars "taxicabs," and at first we regarded driving them as a kind of busman's holiday from the dangers of our other rides. But the pressure from the factories was relentless; executives who headed up the programs dreamed of huge bonuses one moment and feared for their jobs the next. The term taxicab was soon taboo. What few of us grasped at the time was that the Trans-Am would have such staying power, that 40 years later, for example, there would be a Trans-Am vintage series with full fields and fans content to witness a mere simulacrum of the original. (Now, finally, my old Challenger gets to feel what it's like to win, thanks to the superb driving of its owner, Ken Epsman.)

The emphasis on the manufacturers masked how critical the driver was. In many ways, the Trans-Am was the best test of driving ability of any series of that era. Finesse, fitness, car control—it took all that, but it also called for using the car as a battering ram; it was a rare race that didn't see us finish with a bent spoiler or deep gouges in the doors.

The races took over three hours, and because the engines were up front, the cockpits were so hot that you could sweat off ten pounds. The exhaust pipe ended right under the driver's door, and halfway through the race you'd be totally deaf. The ride was harsh, the brake-pedal effort high. Pit stops offered no relief, as they only took about 15 seconds. The great designer Colin Chapman once said that rules are for the interpretation of wise men and the obedience of fools. In the Trans-Am, cheating was widespread and never posed a moral dilemma; in fact, it was often the source of entertainment. The SCCA sanctioned the series, and their officials weighed the top three cars after each race. If you were running below the minimum weight limit—and many were—one popular gambit was to use the post-race confusion to mask a lightning-fast change of all four wheels—to four whose tires were filled with water. George Follmer had a helmet full of lead that a crewman would substitute for the real one—the joke being that the lead and George's head were much the same thing. And then there were the secret fuel tanks—ours, good for an extra lap or two, was cleverly hidden under the dashboard. In addition to cheating, we were obliged to lie. Chrysler's rep made it clear that I was never to admit to a blown engine. Never. Suppose we had just put a rod through the side of the block and were coasting to a stop, pouring smoke; my job was to be ready with something else to blame, and I actually kept a list of possibilities in the back of my mind. No writer was ever fooled, but the whole charade seemed to satisfy our bosses in Detroit.

Our mission at Autodynamics was to support AAR. In Chrysler's eyes, we were to tag along, accepting whatever secondhand technology AAR handed down to us. Our lowly status was confirmed when the car colors were assigned. AAR was given an elegant dark blue, while we were stuck with a bilious shade of green. Dodge was calling it Sublime—our crew called it Puke Green. I had the hood and roof painted flat black and designed oversized, NASCAR-style numbers, and in the end we managed to cover up quite a lot of the green. It could have been worse. Chrysler was the last of the major manufacturers to get on the pony car band wagon, and they were trying painfully hard to be hip; in addition to Sublime, Dodge brochures offered purple (Plumb Crazy) and orange (Go-Mango). The color affair ordinarily wouldn't have been a big deal, but in the chemistry of the moment, it got our guys pissed off about how we were supposed to defer to AAR, and we became determined to beat them. Beat Your Teammate is a familiar mantra in racing, and now it was our goal. No reflection on Dan Gurney; he was a hero to every man on our team. But that didn't keep us from wanting to beat AAR. In fact, our zeal led to a mistake that would come to haunt us.

An early—illegal—step in building the car involved submerging the body in a large tank filled with acid. The acid ate at the metal, thereby thinning it and saving some weight. We spied on AAR and found out how long their 'Cuda was in the tank, and made sure the Challenger was in it longer.

"Longer" was too long. The first race was at Laguna Seca, and when the tech inspector leaned casually on the roof it gave way, making a small dent. The inspector told us we'd have to have a new roof by the next morning, or we wouldn't be allowed to qualify. What to do? Steal a car off the street? Believe me, we were so wound up, we considered it. Instead, we rushed to the local Dodge dealer, who looked a little blank until we called Detroit, then suddenly he was all smiles and cheerfully surrendered a car right from his showroom floor. That was the power of a Trans-Am team in 1970.

We cut the roof off our borrowed car and welded it onto the race car—an all-night job, but we even managed to get it painted. Unhappily, the acid dipping had made the entire car brittle, and every time we ran, cracks opened up that were big enough for me to see through the floor to the track. Our welder spent hours patching things up. Several races went by before we were able to complete a second, undipped car. It was better, but stiffening the frame exacerbated the car's other weakness: the geometry of the rear suspension. As I braked for certain turns, the rear brakes locked up, causing the axle assembly to jump from side to side, leaving skid marks on the track. All I could do was to brake gently, which of course let anyone following me right by. The brakes cost us an easy win at Elkhart Lake in midsummer. Our engine that day was so strong that on Elkhart's long straights I easily passed Mark Donohue's Javelin, then Parnelli Jones's Mustang, to take the lead. But the axle began to skip around again, and I had to settle for third. At that point in the season we were neck and neck with AAR, but Swede Savage finished second at Elkhart, and AAR pulled ahead of us in the points. Chrysler had just told us that for 1971 they would be cutting the team that finished lower in the championship. At the time, we didn't know—and they didn't either—that they would wind up cutting both teams. I'm often asked who was the Trans-Am's best driver. If I were to pick a team, I'd choose Donohue to test the car and get it set up. Then I'd sign Jones to race it. A 1970 Trans-Am car was the result of six years of development, much of it by Mark himself, and along the way it had become a highly specialized object that very few people really understood. The technology of other forms of racing wasn't much help; the cars were lighter than oval-racing stock cars, heavier than a sports car or any of the single-seaters; the races were shorter than an endurance race, but longer than a sprint. Mark had an uncanny feel for these often-conflicting factors. Many of his early successes with Roger were in the Trans-Am. He identified with the series; it was in his DNA. It helped a lot that he was a graduate engineer and that he spoke the language of engineering. All the bright guys at GM's think tank liked to work with him.

Parnelli Jones was Mark's natural rival. It was Mark the good guy vs. Parnelli the spoiler, the hired gun: tough, mean, glowering, a man who wouldn't hesitate to put you off the road, especially if your name was Donohue. Anyhow, that was Parnelli's race face. Turns out he was super smart and even a bit sentimental. But in the car—and this is the reason I'd pick him over Mark—he very simply put the pedal to the metal harder than anyone, and kept it down longer. He was a force out there, and slower cars scattered the moment he appeared in their mirrors.

His greatest drive was at Riverside, the last race of 1970. With about 15 laps to go, Parnelli was forced off the road by a backmarker who hadn't seen him coming. He shot into the desert at 160 mph, lashed the car around among the boulders and ditches, and regained the track, trailing dust and gravel, the front of his car pushed in. His teammate, George Follmer, had a 20-second lead. It was going to be a Ford 1-2, confirming the series championship they had already clinched. Most of the spectators had left, and the smog was oozing up from the valley below, a kind of man-made dusk. But Jones was slicing through the gloom in his school-bus-yellow Mustang, its sides now streaked with oil.

George had many of Parnelli's characteristics—especially the threatening aura—and he, too, was successful in other forms of racing. He would be my pick for third-best Trans-Am driver of all time. But on this day, Parnelli was in a world of his own. I didn't see the pass, but one moment George was still out front and the next, like magic, it was Parnelli. During that summer a tectonic shift took place in the industry: The pony car market suddenly lost its momentum. The manufacturers reacted swiftly, canceling contracts right and left—including AAR's and ours. Of the factory teams, only Javelin would be back in 1971, and their victory was both overwhelming and totally meaningless. As for us, we won our private battle with AAR, which should have meant a great deal, but which meant nothing at all to anyone.

Fittingly, the Challenger broke down early at Riverside, and I was standing in the pits when the race ended and the cars began to trickle in. Hunter Thompson once wrote about a great wave sweeping up a beach, leaving a high-water mark where it finally broke and rolled back. Parnelli's drive that late afternoon in the desert at Riverside was the high-water mark, and when the wave rolled back, it took the Trans-Am, in all its glory and frenzy, with it.

Introduction for Road Racing Drivers Club Honoree: Parnelli Jones

LONG BEACH, CALIFORNIA, APRIL 15, 2010

His senses knew where the edge was and his personality told him to be on it, all the time and everywhere. His car perfectly balanced, his rivals pushed not quite off the road, but almost. He was always where the action was. He was the first over 150 mph at Indy, the first big-name driver to challenge the Baja, the top driver of the Trans-Am in its iconic year, 1970.

A driver is measured by the company he keeps, and Parnelli battled with the very best. Dan Gurney. Mark Donohue. A. J. Foyt. George Follmer, Jim Clark, Mario Andretti—his opponents a who's who of racing greats from all branches of the sport.

He was incredibly versatile. He drove everything from midgets to sprint cars, Indy cars, and stock cars. He has raced up Pikes Peak and down the Baja Peninsula. He has raced on dirt, on the high banks, on road courses from Riverside to Road America to Lime Rock. He had so much talent he needed to test it in every way possible.

Much of his career is the history of racing itself. He won Indy in the twilight of the roadster era, and lost it in a machine that was years ahead of its time. He became a car owner, and Al Unser drove his cars to victory at Indy—twice. But it wasn't only his record that has made Parnelli stand out; it is Parnelli, the man. He looks tough, ready for a fight, but his real weapon is his intelligence—on the track, where he made so few mistakes, and off it, where his business sense, along with a little help from his partner, Vel Miletich, and a few dozen Firestone tire stores, has made him rich.

He is the proud father of P. J. and Page, themselves drivers of distinction.

The kid from Texarkana, Arkansas, may have left us in his dust, but he cannot escape our respect—or our affection.

Rufus Parnelli Jones could look mean, scary mean, but the facts show he never pushed people off the road, never did any of the things mean people do. He just beat you and beat you again, and he did it so often, you had to conclude he was mean.

My first job in TV was with ABC, and I was incredibly lucky that I had Jim McKay as a mentor and friend. Watching him in action was the best possible education I could have had. Jim wrote the iconic tease ("thrill of victory, agony of defeat") that opened every Wide World of Sports—*and several hundred more, all classics. Before he got into TV he had been a newspaper reporter, and he believed that this taught him how to prioritize his ideas—and, especially, how to keep things short. When he went into semiretirement I inherited shows that he, typically, would have done, such as the Tour de France, the Ironman, and the Baja 1000. Each has its own distinct character. For example, the Iditarod—a favorite of mine—is about the cold, the dogs, and the courage of the mushers. In that order. Here are a couple of my teases, written somewhere between Anchorage and Nome.*

Iditarod I, '89–'90

A journey of a thousand miles must begin with a single step. In the journey called the Iditarod, that first step and the countless millions that follow it are the steps of dogs, their paw prints tracing a nearly invisible trail across the snowy wilderness of Alaska. Eleven hundred miles, eleven days, maybe more, this journey lasts. The men and women who race the Iditarod must be full of courage and toughness and know-how. It can be violent for them along this trail: steep ravines coated in ice, or maybe at 60 below with howling wind. But it can be quiet, too, and in the stillness of the frozen air, you can listen for the ghosts of the past and the sounds of the great gold rush days. It is a journey into the twilight of exhaustion when the body slows down and the brain plays tricks. How do you act then, when your guard is down? You learn a lot about yourself in this race, and that hard-won knowledge comes as one step follows another.

Iditarod II, '89–'90

The unvarying routines, the hard work and the harsh cold, your dependence on the dogs and theirs on you, produce the framework for a world all its own—a world in which rest is rare and uncomfortable and sleep is shallow, because you fear you might get left behind. It is a world in which life means motion and reality is the trail ahead, and a half-formed idea of the finish line in a faraway place called Nome. It is a world of silence and ice—ice under your feet, ice stretching to the horizon, ice on your face as your exhaustion deepens with the cycle of the days and your world shrinks to a tight cocoon. Your time becomes detached from real time, and finally, even the haunting beauty of Alaska goes unseen. The repetitive, dreamlike quality of life on the trail can almost mask the fact that the race is even going on.

Three of the F1 circuits are located in places that have historical significance. Two date from World War II—Silverstone was a bomber base, and Spa saw fighting during the Battle of the Bulge. The third—Singapore—was founded early in the 19th century as a trading post for the East India Company. In a sense, the race is a modern-day export, its value enhanced by running the race at night so that it can be seen live in Europe at a civilized time.

Singapore '09

F1, at night: an illicit pleasure, the senses assaulted by flashing bursts of sparks and flames, by the salt smell of the dark sea, by memories of this place as a distant outpost of the British Empire.

Fifteen hundred bulbs, 2,000 watts each, turn the hot, humid, equatorial night into a world half dream, half real. Singapore: halfway around the world from the last race, day and night inverted, drivers, disoriented, trying to stay on European time, going to bed at dawn.

From the cockpit, the scene is surreal: the light unnaturally the same at every point along the lap; the world beyond the track: black, invisible. Even the shadows swept away in this cleanest of all cities.

The turns are slow but tricky, the pavement rough, the curbs high, the trolley tracks uneven. This is a place where mistakes get made.

F1 at night—a kind of theater, a defiance of nature, an experience not to be missed.

The lights are on, the cars are ready. The Grand Prix of Singapore is . . . *next!*

Most of the articles chosen for this book were first printed by Road & Track. *An exception is the following, which was printed by* Sports Illustrated *and later condensed for* Reader's Digest.

Le Mans is like Monaco and Indy, an event attended by people who don't go to any other race, and this wider audience opens the door to writing about the event from unusual angles. At Sports Illustrated, *Bob Brown asked me to describe what it was like to drive Le Mans at night.*

Down a Dark Hall at 185 mph

SPORTS ILLUSTRATED, NOVEMBER 15, 1976

The 24 Hours of Le Mans is a monument to the idea that life goes on. It is a French national institution dating back more than half a century, with a quarter of a million devotees turning out every June for a scene that perhaps can be compared only to the Woodstock rock festival. But to the driver, speeding through the night portion of the race in a vehicle that is about as sturdy as an eggshell, with lights as useful at 200 mph as miners' lamps, the idea that life will go on—or that the night will ever end—doesn't seem the least bit certain.

At any time, day or night, Le Mans is an imposing circuit. Its many fast turns permit laps of an extremely high average speed but, because the track is narrow and lined with guardrails, the sensation is of aiming your car down a twisting hallway. A lap is 8.36 miles long and takes you through the rural countryside on the outskirts of the railhead town of Le Mans, 135 miles southwest of Paris. Most of the circuit consists of main roads ordinarily open for public use, and as you rip past fields and farmhouses and occasionally plunge through dense pine forests, you are in fact rushing from one small Le Mans suburb to another. Mulsanne is one of these towns. Arnage is another. At racing speeds, however, you rarely notice the scenery.

I wrote this article for *Sports Illustrated* in 1976, and it was an assignment I knew from the beginning was going to be fun. "Write about driving at night at Le Mans," Bob Brown said—adding that he wanted the article three days after the race, so it would run in the next issue.

At night there's almost nothing to see except the road. Cars are no longer recognizable by their shapes or colors; they are just twin dots of light. The few illuminated landmarks that do exist surge at you out of the darkness in an endless repetitive sequence. The pits. The carnival at the Esses. The cafe that's one-third of the way along the straight leading from Le Mans out to Mulsanne. The rest of the lap becomes abstract; rows of bright reflectors along both sides of the road outline the route clearly, but make it look more like a lighted diagram than a race circuit. In this way the night conceals many of the specific hazards of the course, replacing a sense of coming and going from particular danger points with a pervasive uneasiness.

Half of a Le Mans driver's night is spent on the track, the other half, trying to get some sleep while his co-driver is out with the car. The more organized teams rent trailers behind the pits as dormitories for their drivers, and in the eight years I have done the race, I have always gone to my trailer knowing I must sleep to keep my reflexes working.

But sleep has never been easy to come by.

In the darkness of the trailer I see images of the road rushing at me, as if all those laps have been stamped on my mind, a tape loop that cannot be shut off. If I close my eyes, a second later I'm grabbing for the edge of the cot, convinced I'm falling; hours of violent motion in a car have upset my balance. Every year the trailer walls seem thinner, or else the cars are louder, and the roaring is a reminder that my car is out there somewhere. When I am particularly tired I get the idea that the car is still going not so much because the nuts and bolts are right, but because the whole team is willing it to run—sheer mind over matter. For me to sleep is to reduce by one the force that keeps the car going.

One year, 1970, I spent my hours in the trailer half convinced I would not live through the night. That was the year it rained for 20 of the 24 hours. Rain is frightening even on a slow track in broad daylight. At night, driving through Le Mans' fast turns and down the long Mulsanne straight, it is terrifying. On the water-soaked track the tires of my Ferrari aquaplaned uncontrollably, the steering wheel sometimes being wrenched back and forth in my hands and sometimes going dead. Seen from the cockpit the rain didn't fall; it came at me horizontally.

Drivers usually remain at the wheel for three hours or more during the night, allowing their co-drivers a chance to rest, but in the rain that year the concentration required was so great that no one could stay on the track for more than 90 minutes at a stretch. I made so many trips back to the trailer I lost count. Each time I took with me fresh memories of disaster, of fires burning around the track, wrecked cars crammed against guardrails, shiny slickers of rescue workers visible in the headlights, a flag marshal dead at the chicane.

In 1976 the Le Mans night was different. It was humid, the air hanging heavy and close, promising another day as hot as the one we had just had. But it was clear—no chance of rain. I was driving for the

BMW team, and at one a.m. I was between stints at the wheel. I was lying on a cot in one of our trailers. It was too hot to close the windows, and the sound of the cars penetrated the trailer at irregular intervals, unusually loud. An hour before, having just completed a long period in the car, I had enjoyed a compulsive, overwhelming need to replace lost liquids and had overdone it, gulping three quarts of mineral water. I felt bloated, and my thick fireproof underwear was hot and sweaty, but I was too tired to pull it off.

In the opposite corner of the trailer, sleeping soundly, was a German girl, hired by BMW as a hostess for our hospitality camper. The previous afternoon she had been a whirlwind of activity as she made sandwiches and served drinks.

"You'd better take it easy if you're planning to be up all night," I had said to her. "It doesn't matter," she had answered, laughing. "Your cars will break down early." But they hadn't—or rather, mine hadn't; the other three BMWs were out.

As I lay in the trailer I thought back to the start of the race, which seemed a very long time ago. I remembered being on the grid, in all the color and sunlight, posing for pictures in front of the car, clowning with my co-driver to relieve the tension. And I remembered the first lap, racing down the Mulsanne straight, the cars weaving in and out. We all had energy to spare, then.

I got up carefully, so as not to wake the girl, and crossed the compound to the team camper. It was empty, its lights on. I poured some coffee. In the distance I could hear robust German drinking songs coming from a dance hall on the carnival midway beyond the pits. It was almost time for my next turn at the wheel. You could be back home in California, I told myself, lying on the lawn, listening to the Pacific Ocean.

The dark paddock was crowded with the shadowy forms of the transporters. Here and there an oil-streaked car, out of the race, sat lifeless under a tarpaulin. At the concrete steps marking the back entry to the pits, a guard moved out of my way and nodded deferentially. I returned his nod with gravity, caught for a moment by a sense of mission. There was duty still to be done. A race to finish. As I walked up the narrow corridor immediately behind the pits there was a strong smell of racing oil in the air. I was feeling fine.

In the pit the team manager greeted my arrival with indifference, as if I weren't anything other than a mechanism that had come to replace the mechanism currently behind the wheel. I ducked under the refueling hoses that hung from the low ceiling and pulled out my equipment bag. A minute later I was ready, aware of my breathing inside my helmet. Across the track from the pits the grandstand was nearly empty, and in the quiet between the passing of the race cars tinny music played over the public-address system, sounding lonely and vacant. There are very few witnesses to a driver's night stint at Le Mans.

The car came in, suddenly displacing the dark in front of the pits with lights and a cloud of steam. My co-driver emerged, shouting something to me that I couldn't hear, and then I was down in the cockpit, struggling with the harnesses. I saw the signal to start the car and in a moment I was moving up the pit lane. Then the lights of the grandstand were gone and there was only the pool of my own lights ahead of me on the track.

The first lap was awkward and disjointed as the new tires, cold and slippery to begin with, began to heat up with the friction of the track. Then they were hot and sticky, and the car was gripping surely and predictably. I drove in a groove that I had developed during my earlier shifts behind the wheel, guiding the car with an economy of physical movement.

The tense effort of the daylight hours soon gave way to reflexive motions and intuitive thoughts. The miles spun off in an endless journey. The lighted Ferris wheel beside the track seemed to turn as if it were geared mysteriously to the cars revolving on the track. And after six or seven laps, I felt the reestablishment of a strange sense of being in a giant orbit around a central point.

On my trips down the three-mile-long Mulsanne straight I could feel the power releasing itself through the car as it picked up speed second by second. By a quarter of the way along, the car was established in a snug envelope of air that tugged at its sides, making it dart from side to side like an express train on a rough roadbed. The cafe went by on the left, a sustained flash of warm light seen out of the corner of my eye.

When there were other cars on the straight I would duck into the vacuum behind them for a few seconds before passing. In those moments the view up the straight would be cut off. Full speed, and all I could see was six feet, into the back of the car ahead. The Porsches had turbochargers: Their exhausts glowed red with heat, and from under their wheels the passing lines painted on the road came spitting out like tracer bullets.

At other tracks you are still accelerating when it comes time to brake at the end of the straight, but the Mulsanne is so long that the car comes to a stage where its power simply cannot push any more air out of its way, and the speed levels off. Terminal velocity. Alone on the straight, that was 185 mph in my BMW, but it became higher, more than 190, when I could tuck into another car's slipstream. The speed produces neither giddiness nor fear, but a sense of a transfer of power, the car's power into my hands and arms.

The instruments glowed green in the dark. The guardrail reflectors streamed by like twin strings of bright pearls. The engine droned, straining against the night air. I shifted a little in the seat, aware of my sweat-soaked suit. I felt warm, mellow. Consciousness was a dark hollow of convexity, and the car was alive.

Three reflecting signs mark the approach of the Mulsanne kink, where the road dives to the right. It isn't as much a turn as a swerve; it can be taken flat out, but only with perfect timing. Just after the signs the road rises under the car as if the macadam has drawn a deep breath. This points the nose of the car up, and at that moment you must initiate the turn while your lights are elevated into the trees beyond. You turn into the darkness, every lap requiring the faith that you will do it at the right instant, and that there will be no oil on the track.

The signs came up, then were gone behind me in the dark. I felt the road lift under the car and saw the lights point into the trees. A camber change in the road started the steering wheel to the right. For one beat, my hands resisted the turning, then followed it through with a wrist movement of great gentleness, almost a caress. At such speed the car reacted as if it had glanced off an invisible wall. With no sense of duration, and with no awareness of having been in the turn, I was rushing down the ensuing straight on a new heading.

Isolated two-thirds along a straight that takes hardly any skill to drive, the Mulsanne kink is one of the most difficult turns in racing, its difficulty increasing greatly at night. Even drivers of comparatively slow cars have been killed instantly by crashes at the kink. This year a French driver died there in a car with a top speed of little over 150 mph. I have always driven cars much faster than that, and to see the trees go by at 185 mph or more, just a few feet away, erases from your mind even the most subconscious trickle of any idea that you might survive if something went wrong.

In most parts of a race track, even Le Mans, you picture a crash and you imagine you might have a chance to survive it. You might have to pry yourself out of the car or try to hold your breath in a fire, but some sort of chance would exist. Having no chance at all is unusual, and I have always wondered if there wouldn't be a certain majesty to that millisecond when you knew it was coming, and knew it with such certitude that you didn't even brace yourself for the struggle, or wince at the impending pain. I don't know. But I have noticed, leaving the kink behind, a perceptible tingling, the reawakening of my nerve endings.

After almost a minute at full speed, braking for the hairpin at the end of the Mulsanne comes like a period of reentry into a real world. All during the time the car lost speed, I sat there, oddly weightless, foot hard on the brake pedal, my eyes watching as the edges of the road came back into focus. The smell was of the brake pads, acrid and burning. My foot, which has some broken bones in it from a crash of another time, ached from the effort. Then, as if the energy had been torn out of it by the braking, the car rounded the hairpin and weakly began to gather speed toward Arnage.

So it went, the night and the fatigue combining so that the usual frames of reference gradually slipped away or became meaningless, leaving me with bright pinpoint vision in an existence that occupied only the single dimension of speed. Until with no warning a lap came where I swung the car onto the Mulsanne and knew something wasn't the same.

Slowly I turned my head to the left, peering through the window. There on the horizon, a long crayoned line of deep red signaled the dawn.

Within two laps I could see faint particles of light through the trees. Soon after that I could see the other drivers in their cars, shadows in rival cockpits, concentrated forces that, as I had, had made it through the night. Of course each was a threat now to my success in the race, but there was still that moment of kinship, the cheery wave as I went by.

In the pits when my stint was over there were smiles all around. Want some breakfast? How's it going? I thought of walking up to the trailer again, but sleep could wait. It was good to talk to the reporters, who looked fresh after sleeping at their hotels. The stands were filling with people again.

Ten hours still stretched ahead before the finish. Repeatedly we fought our way into top positions only to be delayed by nagging mechanical problems. My laps around the nearly empty, trash-strewn track had a dreamlike quality, shaded always by the fear that even at the last moment something might go wrong and our whole effort would be for nothing. To survive the night and then not last the race would be a bewildering injustice. The car just had to finish.

And in the last laps, when the crowd was emptying over the guardrails onto the track, exuberant, waving, and the marshals were waving their flags like semaphores, and the car felt strong under me, I knew we had it made. We had finished. In 24 hours we had gone 2,565 miles, 306 times around the same 8 miles. And we had come in 10th. Suddenly I realized I couldn't remember what the night had been like, couldn't remember at all.

While *Sports Illustrated* wanted me to focus on night driving at Le Mans, *Road & Track* wanted the entire experience—the story of the race in the context of life during the days leading up to it.

Road & Track's *idea for this article was the exact opposite of what* Bob Brown *had in mind for* Sports Illustrated *the year before. R & T wanted to give the reader a sense not only of the race itself, but of the days leading up to it—the whole Le Mans experience.*

This was almost 30 years ago, when the Mulsanne straight was still three miles long and cars were designed for top speed; the Ferrari 512 S I drove in 1970 went 240 mph, and the Porsche 917s were even faster. The organizers thought this was too fast, so a pair of chicanes was built along the Mulsanne to slow things down. Overnight, the emphasis changed to handling and braking. Today, top speeds are around 220 mph.

Through the years there have been many detail improvements, but to the driver, the core experience—the four-hour tech inspection, the practice sessions that don't end until midnight, the old hotel that doesn't have air-conditioning—all that is much the same.

Le Mans means different things to different people, but it has a magnetic attraction that has universal appeal.

Le Mans—24 Hours
ROAD & TRACK, OCTOBER 1977

The first requirement for a driver at Le Mans is to appear at scrutineering at the time his car is there. For each team there is a different appointment time. The cars pass slowly through a dozen checkpoints, being measured, weighed, filled with fuel, emptied of fuel, prodded and poked. Meanwhile, the team's drivers present their medical cards, licenses, and insurance papers. Le Mans scrutineering can take more than four hours, but the inspectors themselves, glacially formal Frenchmen wearing dark ties and blue suits, seem to relish the tedium.

When everything has been approved, the team is photographed for posterity by a battery of photographers representing publications from all over the world. Our Renault Mirages were posed with French and American flags that symbolized the cooperation between Renault, which made our engines, and our Phoenix-based team. In other contemporary forms of racing, commercialism is everything, but at Le Mans no one begrudges you a touch of patriotism.

First Practice

There are only two practice sessions for Le Mans, but each is six hours long. The first runs from 6:00 p.m. to midnight Wednesday; the second from 5:00 to 11:00 p.m. Thursday. Thanks to long summer evenings, it's light until 10:00 p.m., and there's a nice balance between daylight and night running. This year rain was threatening as practice began. It was still dry at the pits, but after a while cars started coming by streaked with water. The word was that it was raining toward the end of the long Mulsanne straight.

Ordinarily I am not afraid to race in the rain, but I am afraid at Le Mans. I don't mind going through the slow parts of the track in the rain; but when I'm going 180 mph or more and the car is aquaplaning and I can't see properly, *that* makes me worry. Also, I drove in the 1970 race when rain came down relentlessly for 20 of the 24 hours, numerous cars were wrecked, a corner worker was killed, and conditions were so bad that the winner, Hans Herrmann, announced immediately afterward that he was retiring from racing. So when I see rain at Le Mans, I tense up reflexively.

But this year the rain played only a minor role. The shower at the beginning of practice dried off well before anyone was under pressure to go really fast, and the track stayed dry until another shower that came at dawn in the race. At that point only Jacky Ickx took any real risks. It could be argued that he was the only driver on the track at the time in a strategic position, which justified chance-taking (he was engaged in a flat-out pursuit of the leading Alpines). But it's probably closer to the truth to say that Ickx drove as he did in the rain because he is one of the few drivers in racing today who seems to thrive on danger.

Second Practice

The second day of practice was clear. Fuel-pump problems stranded both the Mirages far from the pits, but because the cars were radio-equipped, it was possible to find out where they were and send mechanics to make repairs.

Once the cars were running right it became obvious that their top speed was as much as 15 mph slower than the Porsche prototypes and the Renault Alpines. Since we had the same engines as the Alpines, we began to worry that the Mirage's problem was aerodynamic drag. (Ironically, in our testing at Phoenix, we had been able to evaluate almost every part of the car, but the shortness of the Phoenix track kept us from checking the car at top speed.) Trying to reduce drag, we flattened our rear wings, but this made the cars unstable without giving us any more speed. Another problem was extreme wind turbulence in the cockpit.

When practice was over we assessed the situation. After so many months of work and hope it was hard to admit we weren't as fast as we had anticipated. The only solution to our problems seemed to lie in a total redesign of the body, and there obviously wasn't time for that.

At this point, team owner Harley Cluxton displayed his instinct for leadership. During a long dinner at our hotel he extracted from the drivers and the crew every useful bit of information relating to our problems. Then the next morning he met with John Horsman, the team manager, and drew up a plan for what could realistically be done in the time left before the race. The air scoop would be extended to pick up less-turbulent air. Cockpit pressure would be relieved by venting the area behind the driver's head. The front part of the cockpit cowling would be reshaped. None of this work, however, would be allowed to interfere with the regular preparation of the cars. We knew the strong cards held by the other teams were already on display, while ours—fast pit work and a proven chassis—wouldn't be played until the race itself.

Interlude

A feature of the Le Mans schedule is that on Friday, the day before the race, the track is closed in order to give the teams time for the final preparation.

Our team stayed in La Chartre, a small town a half-hour south of the track. On this day it seemed as if the whole life of the town was given over to watching us prepare for the race. Old men and women—many of them carrying long French baguettes, which made them look as if they had stepped straight out of a travel poster—stood immobile for hours at the entrance to our garage. And a steady stream of kids ran back and forth between the garage and the hotel, checking the progress on the cars and hoping to get a driver's autograph.

For the drivers, Friday was a day off, although at one time or another each of us visited the garage to see how things were going. I wandered around town looking in store windows at French pastries and mopeds, everything priced bewilderingly in francs. I also went jogging. The streets were narrow, with old stone sidewalks, and I saw disbelief registering on the faces of the townspeople who saw me galloping by in my shorts and T-shirt.

Every now and then throughout the day I could feel my mind sliding. Instead of being aware of whatever was going on, I'd be thinking about the race.

We're Off

The race didn't start until four p.m., but because of the vast crowds it was necessary to leave for the track around noon. Leaving the hotel I felt as though I was embarking on an expedition, because in addition to all my usual driving equipment, I also took blankets, pillows, and some special food.

The paddock area behind the pits was crowded, and the pits were even more so. The crowds, the noise, the excitement, made the whole thing feel very much like Indianapolis just before the start, but with one important difference: At Indy the start is the beginning of a 500-mile sprint, and in its explosive power it is the logical continuation of the immediate pre-race tension. But at Le Mans the start, really, is nothing. It is merely the moment you put your 24-hour "system" into action. For a handful of drivers—the inexperienced, or a few who, for tactical reasons, are assigned sprinting roles by their teams—the start means going fast, but for everyone else it is as if you are a clock, which, having just been wound, now begins to run smoothly, regularly.

Vern Schuppan and I were side by side at the start, but in a lap it was apparent that his car, which was fitted with stiffer springs, was faster, and gradually he drew away. I was furious that my co-driver, Michel Leclère, and I had made this technical blunder, but it was too late to do anything. On the plus side, however, the revised cockpit cowling sharply reduced the wind buffeting. I was delighted that after several years of driving GT cars at Le Mans I was now back in a full-fledged prototype, with a solid chance to beat my previous best finish (third in 1971, with a Ferrari 512 M), and even had a chance to win.

Every long-distance team has its complements of timers and other supporting personnel, but in the case of our team, Harley had encouraged some of our financial backers to handle these jobs, with the result that we had some extremely intelligent people, including a doctor, a lawyer, and a banker, in the pits. John Horsman had organized this eclectic group, and as team manager he received a constant flow of reports about fuel consumption, tire and brake-pad wear, lap times, and overall standings. In addition, because Renault had asked for regularly updated information about their sensitive turbocharged engines, the drivers radioed reports on boost pressure and exhaust gas temperature, as well as all the regular engine functions.

By eight p.m. the light of the long evening slanted across the track. One Renault Alpine was out, a victim of an early fire, and Ickx's Porsche had also succumbed. The remaining Alpines controlled the race. Our Mirages had moved up to fifth and sixth.

I was headed down the Mulsanne with more than 50 miles to go before a scheduled fuel stop when I noticed the fuel-warning light begin to flicker. Odd. Two hundred miles an hour on the ultra-smooth Mulsanne is a little like being in the cockpit of a low-flying plane, and with a pilot's deliberateness, I checked the instruments. The fuel pressure was correct, and I recalled that our drivers' instruction manual, which I had memorized before the race, said that with the warning light flashing, I should be able to make it to the pits without slackening my pace. Okay. But in a moment the light was on steadily.

I slowed and glanced at the fuel pressure. It was falling. I activated the reserve pump, but the pressure continued to drop. The engine was dying. I coasted around the corner at the end of the straight and pulled off to the side.

In the next two hours, with the aid of a full complement of tools that we carried on board, I checked everything I could, but the fact remained that there were streaks of gas along the underside of the outboard tank, and I was all but certain we had had a leak and I was out for good. Le Mans regulations don't allow refueling on the course.

Eventually someone was sent for me and I took the long, slow ride to the pits via the narrow back road. There John Horsman sensed my crushing disappointment at being out, and asked me to stick around in case a reserve driver was needed for the remaining car. It was at best a tenuous relationship with the team, but I was thankful for it. I couldn't bear to leave.

By then it was 11 p.m., dark, and the Alpines were facing a challenge by Ickx, who, having taken over the second Porsche, was storming through the field. Our remaining Mirage was still fifth. During the night the order remained the same, but the Porsches drew closer to the Alpines. Then, in the early-morning rain, Ickx sliced into third. Just before dawn the first-place Alpine whispered into the pits and died. By noon all three were out. They had dominated the first three-quarters of the race, but at Le Mans minutes can be like hours and hours like months, and by early afternoon, with the crowd having flowed back into the grandstands like a returning tide, it was almost as if the Alpines had been in some other Le Mans, not this one.

The demise of the Alpines put the Porsche of Ickx, Hurley Haywood, and Jürgen Barth firmly in the lead. Our Vern Schuppan / Jean-Pierre Jarier Mirage was second, miles behind, but running so well that I knew I would never be needed as a relief driver, so, early in the afternoon, I walked up the pits toward the first turn.

Looking back along the track toward the Ford chicane, I could see the cars popping into sight at random intervals. They seemed to hang there suspended in the distance before crystallizing into a discernible form, a particular car, which then rushed toward me. Only then could I hear the sound of the engine winding through the wide-spaced gears and the long hesitation on the upshift. The cars seemed freed by then of that earlier urgency when tenths of seconds still mattered. Still, as the cars fled up through that first turn, they transmitted to anyone watching them an unmistakable sense of power generated seemingly without effort.

As I watched them pass, climbing through the long right turn, I could almost imagine I was still driving in the race. Vividly I could feel how it had been to crest that first hill under the Dunlop Bridge and rush steeply down toward the Esses. I could remember how the heavy braking between the earth embankments caused a compression of energy that was released split seconds later as the car catapulted itself along the tiny straight into Tertre Rouge.

The last hours went by with no change as the race drew to a close. Then with less than 40 minutes to go, Haywood brought the leading Porsche into the pits trailing smoke. Holed piston. Le Mans regulations require that in order to be classified as a finisher, a car must be running at the finish and must cross the line under its own power.

The mechanics disconnected the turbo and removed the spark plug from the broken cylinder. Just before four p.m. they sent the cropped car out onto the track. It was a strange time, waiting to see if the Porsche could make it. It seemed that the race had passed beyond the points, where the outcome would be determined by the relative qualities of the men competing in it; instead, it was as though the whole thing was in the hands of fate.

With Jarier in the Mirage for the finish, Harley and I stood with Vern and watched for the Porsche. It reappeared but—too soon! The checkered flag hadn't yet been waved, and now the car was committed to another lap. Vern, who had the most to gain if trouble struck the Porsche, was also the most composed. I was in anguish. As much as I wanted our Mirage to win, and would have done anything I could have to help, I knew that to have been part of the winning team, but not to have driven the car, would undoubtedly be the most frustrating experience of my career.

Then the Porsche came around again, this time to win.

The first Le Mans was held in 1923, and since then it has evolved, step by step, from a way for manufacturers to showcase the toughness of their cars to the present, with its emergent hybrid technology. This article is about Le Mans 16 years ago, a boom time with possibly the strongest-ever entry, and competition so intense that cars were running within a second or two of their qualifying speed.

Run, Rabbits, Run
ROAD & TRACK, SEPTEMBER 1998

Among the great and wholly original races of the world today, Le Mans is right up there with the Monaco Grand Prix, Indy, and the Daytona 500. Each has its own alchemy, but Le Mans alone has late evening light, in northern France, on close to the longest day of the year.

This light is long and low and raking. It takes the green fields and makes them iridescent. It touches the cars and makes them glow. On the 200-mph run out of Mulsanne west to Arnage, it blazes through the windshield, making it painful for a driver to keep his eyes on the road. There are many shadows, but even the shadows seem filled with light.

It is the margin of the day. Already drifting through the sun-warmed air are the cool currents of night. The smoke of campfires mixes with the smells of rubber and oil. In the quiet between the passing of cars, you hear the laughter of children playing games. The race spins its clockwise gyre, its violence and the tranquility of the long, lingering evening held in perfect equipoise.

Oh, sure, some years it rains or is cold, but when you have experienced a classic Le Mans evening, you will remember it always. Indeed, that marvelous northern European light, the light of Monet, the light of Gothic cathedrals, is one of the few things that is constant in a race that is perpetually reinventing itself.

The track itself has undergone three major layout changes, each of which irrevocably altered the basic nature of the event. The original circuit of 1923 was typical for that time: a triangle with three long straights and three hairpins, 11 miles from Le Mans to Mulsanne to Arnage and back to Le Mans, all on public roads. (Near the center was the field where Wilbur Wright made the first powered flight in Europe.) In 1932 they lopped off some straightaway and replaced it with the Dunlop curve, the Esses, and Tertre Rouge, high-speed turns that forced designers to consider handling as well as pure power. With minor changes, this 8.4-mile layout lasted until 1972.

This was the course of Phil Hill, Olivier Gendebien, Mike Hawthorn, and Stirling Moss; of Cunninghams, D Jags, Aston Martins, and Ferraris—always Ferraris; they won six straight in the 1960s. It was the scene of racing's worst disaster, the crash of 1955, in which 80 people were killed. It was where Ford finally beat Ferrari at its own game, and Dan Gurney and A. J. Foyt scored their great win. Starts involved the unforgettable sight of 60 drivers running to their cars. Crowds were huge—over 300,000. Steve McQueen's Le Mans was filmed on this course. The turns at Maison Blanche were the stuff of legend—fast swerves, blind, between the stone walls of centuries-old farmhouses. Young drivers dreamed of winning Le Mans, not a grand prix. Until 1969, there was no guardrail, and patrons of the Hunaudieres Cafe drank Pernod sitting at the edge of the Mulsanne, right where the fast cars shifted into fifth at 200 mph.

It was a fearsome and wonderful track, and it delivered a sensation of speed unmatched by any other course. In 1971 a high-water mark was reached with an entry that included almost 20 Ferraris and long-tailed Porsche 917s, all of which could run 230 mph. Early on, aboard one of the Ferraris, I set the absolute track-record lap (for the moment; it was eventually improved upon), at 151 mph. Driving that fast involved a kind of reckless joy. Down the Mulsanne straight, three miles at full tilt, slicing through fields and woods, a flickering pattern of light and shadow on the road, the speed increasing with a rush, like a released breath. Eight miles in just over three minutes. The winner's record for total distance still stands: 3,315 miles.

The following year, a twisty mile of new track replaced the terrifying Maison Blanche. Safety demanded it, but speeds dropped almost 20 mph, and a lap became more about technique and less about nerve. This was the era of Jacky Ickx, Derek Bell, Henri Pescarolo, Klaus Ludwig, Al Hubert, and Hurley Haywood. Matra and Renault were winners, but it was Porsche that replaced Ferrari as the team to beat; starting in 1976 Porsche won an incredible 10 out of 12. Crowds were smaller, and current Formula One drivers fewer. The organizers, the Automobile Club of the West, became increasingly isolated from motor racing's international governing body, the FIA, devising rules that were for Le Mans only. The length of the race, so integral to its appeal, was a TV turnoff. There was the sense that Le Mans was faltering, becoming a backwater of the sport.

To make matters worse, in 1990, a pair of chicanes was installed in the Mulsanne. Again the change was for safety's sake, but it emasculated the track's greatest remaining feature. In a stroke, the romance of Big Speed was gone.

From a designer's point of view, Le Mans was now just another circuit, albeit a long one that put exceptional strain on the gearbox and brakes. Then Bernie Ecclestone began scheduling his grand prix races to conflict with Le Mans, thereby denying the race the *frisson* of Formula One.

But in the early 1990s, against all odds, Le Mans began to come back. The key was boardroom finance: For a manufacturer, compared to the skyrocketing costs of Formula One, Le Mans was cheap. Spend about $25 million, and you were able to showcase a car that looked (sort of) like what you were selling. Jaguar, Mazda, Peugeot, and McLaren-BMW got on the bandwagon and won, along with Porsche. So many teams wanted in that the organizers began staging a prequalifying day some weeks before the event. A gleaming new steel-and-glass structure, complete with garages, a pressroom, and grandstands, was erected along the pit straight.

Whereas the drivers of the 1980s had mostly been men on their way down, it was now fashionable for a young hot shoe to have a Le Mans credit, especially if it was with a factory team. Current F1 driver Alexander Wurz was "discovered" at Le Mans, and others hoped to be. And as for the race being a shadow of its former self—these new guys hadn't even been born in the '60s, so who cared? If anything, this new generation could co-opt the old magic for themselves.

Which brings us to this year. Factory teams from BMW, Porsche, Mercedes-Benz, Toyota, Nissan, and Chrysler were entered, along with smaller teams from Panoz and Courage, and a high-quality assortment of supporting players, including privately entered Ferraris, Porsches, and McLaren-BMWs. If there had ever been a stronger entry, no one could remember it.

The last two Le Mans had been won by the same Reinhold Joest–entered, Porsche-powered, open sports car—a top performer, but nondescript-looking—and while the rules ostensibly sought parity between the sports and GT classes, some tweaking had tipped the playing field toward the more-glamorous GTs. At the front of the grid it was all GTs, with Bernd Schneider's V8 Mercedes breaking the track record by six seconds, and upsetting Martin Brundle's long-tailed Toyota for the pole. Porsches were fourth and fifth. Sixth went to the fastest of the sports category, BMW's agile roadster, while Joest, struggling with aero problems, could only manage ninth. In GT2, the Chrysler Vipers vaporized the Porsche 911s.

At the start, Brundle and Schneider reached the first turn abreast of each other, with the German shouldering his way through first and hanging on until the Mulsanne. Whereupon Brundle swooped by, so eager to get into the headlines that he was running on half tanks. The race had started at two p.m. instead of the usual four p.m., so there was a long stretch before the onset of evening. In that time, both Mercedes and both BMWs retired, and the race established its pattern: Toyota and Porsche out front, and Nissan panting along behind. The pace was incredible; never in the history of the race had lap times been so close to qualifying times.

At Le Mans knowing how fast to lap, especially in the early stages, is something of a black art. In the 1950s John Wyer, then the Aston Martin team manager, would base his calculations on an incremental improvement over the highest previous winning speed. (For example, in 1955 he ran 4:45s for 106 mph; the previous best was 105.85 mph.) In the 1980s, Porsche's recipe was to take their cars' best time, add three seconds, and run that pace for 15 hours. Only then did they make adjustments.

Over the years, of course, cars have become faster, and they run closer to their qualifying speed. They are mechanically tougher and better tested. In the mid-'80s, teams began using three drivers instead of two, allowing more time for rest. Today's drivers get "physio" (physical therapy) and eat food prepared by expert dietitians. But the heyday of the owner/driver is virtually over; factory teams sign aces only, and are willing to pay for them. The total salary for several of this year's top driving trios exceeded $200,000. Finally, the changes that have made Le Mans safer have also made it possible to take risks drivers would not have taken before. A gravel trap is easier on a car than the wall at Maison Blanche.

As the shadows lengthened, Toyota continued to lead, Brundle's low, red car blazing in the copper light of the setting sun. Impressive, unless you knew that this was an all-new team, that its other two cars had already run into trouble, and that Toyota's only attempt at a 24-hour test had been rained out. Impressive, until you noticed that both factory Porsches were stalking the red car's every move from just out of sight, about 50 seconds back.

Toyota would up the pace; Porsche would match it. Whenever Toyota pitted, Porsche glided silently in behind. Then, just after dark, the lead Toyota lost four laps to transmission trouble, leaving Porsche first and second. That lasted until a rain shower at about three a.m., when

Porsche's young Jörg Müller went off in the car he shared with Uwe Alzen and the veteran of 27 Le Mans, Bob Wollek.

As Müller pitted for a fresh undertray, Wollek watched in agony; he has been second four times, but has never won. Just before dawn, the Allan McNish / Laurent Aiello / Stéphane Ortelli Porsche developed a leak in the cooling system. By eight a.m., however, the leaders were all back in business, eerily in the same order they had been in the afternoon before, except that Brundle had crashed, and the leading Toyota was now the Thierry Boutsen car. Nissans were fourth and fifth, but they had misjudged the pace, playing the tortoise-and-hare game that is out-of-date because everyone must now be a hare.

With less than two hours to go, the Toyota's gearbox quit; it was heartbreaking to see their people trying to fight back the tears. By contrast, there was joy for American fans as Le Mans rookie Bill Auberlen would finish fourth in an aging McLaren-BMW, the Doyle-Risi Racing Ferrari 333 SP would come eighth, winning Prototype honors, and David Donohue (Mark's son) would share the GT2-winning Viper.

This was Porsche's 50th anniversary, and they had approached it by replacing their veterans Boutsen and Hans Stuck with younger men. When Allan McNish, age 28, brought his car across the line for Porsche's 16th win (a Le Mans record), it affirmed that this was a company with both a past, and a future. It was a golden moment in the golden light of northern France.

Introduction for Road Racing Drivers Club Honoree: Brian Redman

LONG BEACH, CALIFORNIA, APRIL 18, 2013

You always read that he's underrated—the Underrated Brian Redman. It is used so frequently, you'd think *Underrated* was his first name and *Brian* his middle name. Where did this idea come from? Who does the rating? What system is used? We'd like to know. Ferrari asked him to drive for them and he turned them down. "You'll never get a second chance with Ferrari," people told him. But four years later Ferrari asked again. Brian accepted, and proved to be as fast as the team's stars, Ronnie Peterson, Jackie Ickx, and Clay Regazzoni. In two years he won seven races in the 312. Yet they say he was underrated. Apparently, not by Ferrari.

He drove Porsche's fearsome 917, won 5 of 10 races in 1969, and more the following year, driving for John Wyer. Paired with the highly touted "Seppi" Siffert, Brian matched his times.

He drove a Chevron in the Springbok series and won six of six.

He drove for Jim Hall and won three consecutive F5000 championships, beating the likes of Mario Andretti and Al Unser.

He won Sebring for BMW in 1975, and three years later he won it again, in a Porsche.

He drove a Lola T600 for Cooke-Woods, winning five races and the 1981 IMSA championship.

But they say he was underrated. Obviously, "they" never had to race him.

Brian's many wins speak for themselves: He is one of the great drivers of his generation. Period. What's more, he achieved it against a backdrop of fear, self-doubt, and frightful pain.

First: the fear. He will tell you in all candor that the Porsche 917 terrified him: 235 mph on the Mulsanne, the car changing lanes without warning, the frames cracking, John Woolfe killed in one. But it should be added that Brian eventually came to grips with the 917, and was fastest of all at the notorious Spa.

He also comes from an era where roughly one out of every three top-line drivers was killed racing—and Brian feared he could be one of them.

Brian was being honored once again, and I wrote something with a surprise ending.

Self-doubt. Brian never doubted his ability, but he was constantly asking himself whether he should be racing at all—and in fact, right in mid-career, he retired and took his family to South Africa to run a dealership. It didn't work out. As a sort of farewell to racing, he entered a race, won it, then won five more, in a row.

Pain. Few drivers have suffered like Brian, who had three major accidents: His face was burned in a Porsche at the Targa Florio; his arm was crushed in a terrifying crash at Spa in an F1 Cooper; and he broke his neck at Saint-Jovite when his car got airborne. Each crash put him in the hospital for weeks—endless stretches of pain and boredom, plenty of time to think about quitting. But as it happens, each crash only worked to strengthen his belief in persistence, his conviction that things will come around if you persevere.

He has persevered, and his exploits in vintage-car racing have made him deeply respected by everyone. And, at age 76, he wins virtually every race he starts. He is at all times accessible, and many of us are privileged to know him as a friend.

On the whole, luck has been with him. He has been married all these years to the fabulous Marion, and he has an irrepressible sense of humor. He can regale you with his impersonations—and then there's the spoon trick.

As we have seen, there are several words that apply to Brian, but there is one that encompasses his raw speed, his qualities as a gentleman, his character-defining persistence, and his love of the sport. One word, summing up the man and his career. One word to replace *underrated* once and for all. One word: Champion.

My wife, Ellen, was making paintings of men and women at work—taxi drivers, cowboys, fishermen, a surgeon, and so on. Workers on an assembly line were high on her list, and Edsel Ford II—whom I knew from my boarding-school days—arranged for us to visit Ford's River Rouge plant. We were so fascinated by the place that we wound up spending several days there.

It was time well spent. Ellen made a large painting, and I wrote the article you see here. It was a privilege to have the kind of access we did—an open door not only to manufacturing today, but also to the glory years of the Rouge, when Henry Ford was revolutionizing industrial America.

Ballet Mechanique

ROAD & TRACK, JULY 1995

I n its halcyon days, around 1925, the Ford assembly plant at River Rouge, near Detroit, Michigan, defined America's industrial age at full blast. Just the look of the place, wreathed in smoke and steam, with ships plying to and from its port and strange conveyor belts crisscrossing against the dark sky, gave Americans the first symbol we could really call our own. Forget the pyramids and the Parthenon; we had the Rouge.

The Rouge was American, too, in its energy and self-sufficiency, a giant sprawling complex that answered Henry Ford's instinct to have full control over every part of his product. It made its own steel from iron ore arriving aboard Ford-owned freighters. Rubber for tires came from Ford's rubber plantations in South America. Ford owned hardwood forests and mines; he made his own plate glass. Whatever raw materials were required, Ford bought them at the source, and the Rouge turned them into cars. Or tractors. Or, in the war years, Jeeps and even sub chasers. Given a moment to retool, the Rouge, it seemed, could build anything.

Ellen and I became fascinated by Ford's River Rouge plant, and spent several days there. She wound up making a huge painting of the assembly line. Her painting captures the feeling of the place in a way words cannot, but I found some opportunities for words, too.

Today these glories are past. Centralization on such a vast scale no longer works for Ford, and the company is hacking away at the Rouge. The immense cranes that once unloaded the ships are being dismantled. The steel plant has been sold off. The workforce is about one-fifth of what it once was. Yet the heart of the place, the assembly line, is still churning away, and the cars being made—Mustangs—are part of Ford mythology, and also one of its hottest current models. The aging Rouge is running overtime, with orders backlogged six months. You want a Mustang? It'll be coming from the Rouge; it's the only place they're made.

I visited the Rouge recently with my wife, Ellen, an artist currently painting industrial subjects. Tom Kish, of Ford Public Affairs, acted as our guide. He took us first to the steelmaking facility, now owned by Rouge Steel, where Paul McClure showed us around. Then we went to the assembly line. Our day was almost a biblical journey, beginning with fiery cauldrons of molten steel and ending as we watched cars coughing to life.

We arrived on a rainy morning. There is no vista of the plant or special entry gate that allows you to have a single defining image of the place. It's a landscape of man-made structures designed for function alone. Enormous steel-framed sheds, smokestacks, gantries, storage tanks, ladders, louvered vents, and chain-link fences are all seen as a collage, tightly cropped, nothing visible in its entirety. It is an industrial wilderness that was once our young nation's latest new frontier, replacing the West of the late 19th century.

Ever see steel being made? Rouge Steel's three towering blast furnaces (once nicknamed Henry, Benson, and Edsel, after Mr. Ford's three sons) are in continuous use, 24 hours a day, protected against being shut down, even during a strike, by a special agreement with the steelworkers' union.

Standing on the operations floor of the largest of the furnaces, about three stories aboveground, you see flames pouring from a hole in the furnace's side. Graphite dust sparkling like light snow mixes in the air with iridescent vapors. Molten iron oozes along a brick-lined trough to a hole in the floor. A hollow roar, so loud you have to shout to be heard above it, blows from the furnace. Men dressed in thick clothes move slowly, with stylized indifference to the danger. It is 2,700 degrees in the furnace, but I was told it is bitterly cold on the open-sided operations floor when the winter wind blows in off Lake Erie. It is a primitive world, basically unchanged since Ford built its first furnace there in 1921.

Molten iron leaving the blast furnace is many steps from being, say, a fender. As it passes from one giant building to another, being refined, rolled, and stamped, enormous forces and Brobdingnagian equipment come into play. A 300-ton crane. A ladle 20 feet high. A private railroad. A 3,200-degree oven. The men who run the machines are dwarfed by them, yet they have absolute control. It's their volcano, and they know how it works.

After Rouge Steel, where the interior spaces are vast and dimly lit, almost sepulchral, the assembly line was bright and busy, a compressed space with a low ceiling, crowded with people, car parts, and machines. Almost anywhere you look something is in motion; indeed, movement is the essence here, not the cars. The cars exist, whole, only long enough to be driven outside. Inside, everything is in a state of *becoming*.

The Dearborn Assembly Plant, or DAP, as it is known, was built in 1918 according to the designs of industrial architect Albert Kahn, who once said his buildings were 90 percent business and 10 percent art. Ford took the DAP, which is basically a box, 1,700 feet long, put his assembly line in it, then animated the line according to the principles set forth in the time-motion study by his contemporary, Frederick Winslow Taylor. The simplicity of this beginning is rivaled only by the complexity of what it has wrought.

The DAP, today, is jammed with conveyor belts, pipes, hydraulic lines, ducts, fans, metal cases, flashing lights, and sparks. Evidence of retrofitting and change is everywhere. The line itself twists and turns, doubling back repeatedly in search of more room to accommodate the extra steps involved in more-complex cars. Feeder lines, moving overhead, bring in parts from unseen sources. The aisles are filled with hurrying forklifts and tricycles. Warnings are everywhere, stenciled in black on school-bus yellow. There is a lot of bare metal, silvery in the halogen lighting, then brilliant beneath the welder's torch.

Sirens scream in far-off reaches of the plant. You hear buzzers and the rattle of chains. Air wrenches whine, phones ring. There is music: rock, rap, and country western, seeping muted from the headphones of men and women on the line. Under your feet are wood cobbles, dark and worn with age. (Could Henry Ford have walked here?) A warm breeze is stirred by old fans.

The DAP is a strangely lush place, ripe with a sense of the past while cozily providing those who work in it today with everything needed to do the job, even the right amount of time. But to the visitor, the complexity of it all can be overwhelming. I found myself remembering an exhibit at the Henry Ford Museum where my son, John, and five other kids had formed a very basic assembly line and built a small wooden Model T. First came the chassis (a plain block of wood), then the axles and wheels, and so on. It was all so simple! I decided I might understand things better if I went to the beginning of the Mustang's line and followed it from there.

I was shown to a quiet, cloistered area where large wire cages are filled with stamped-steel parts. Two of these, spot-welded together, begin the subframe, but because many parts—including the engine and transmission—come fully assembled from other plants, a single starting point just doesn't exist. Like the source of a river, it's multifarious. Once the assembly process is under way, however, it takes 20 hours and involves two 10-hour shifts, 1,000 men and women each; 3,500 parts (or more; the engine is counted as one part) are used. At the end of a typical 20-hour day, more than 800 cars have been built.

The line moves at 0.5 mph. At a workstation, you have about a minute to do your thing, whether it be welding, fitting, grinding, wiring, or inspecting. Ergonomics have been perfected to the point that tools and machines are seamless extensions of their users. Some machines have even earned names. The Bad Bug envelops the embryonic chassis and zaps it with 150 welds. The Engine Stuffer lifts the engine from below the car and thrusts it into place.

In the first hours, the chassis slowly emerges, an anonymous, abstract object composed of equally anonymous parts. Only the trained eye can tell which side is up. At roughly the 4-hour mark, the quarter panels are welded in place; at 7 hours, the fenders are bolted on. Painting begins at 9 hours, and is finished 5 hours later, at 14 hours. Trimming (instruments, wiring, windshield, etc.) sees the car moving toward the Fantasy Island loop, where, at 18 hours, the Engine Stuffer installs either a 5.0-liter V8 (made in Cleveland) or a V6 (made in Canada). The seats are among the last parts to be fitted (around the 19-hour mark), and then the car is on the line's final straight, being checked and gassed. Here the assembly line seems broad, leisurely, like a river heading for the sea. The cars gleam.

As each is started and driven away, you wonder: Where is it going? What kind of a life will it have? It is sobering to realize that some of these cars may outlive the plant in which they are made. The DAP's hourly production of about 42 cars does not compare favorably with newer, more-automated plants, which are capable of up to 75 cars per hour. Doubtless there is much about the aging Rouge that is a headache for Ford; it is, after all, just a tool, and ultimately tools outlive their usefulness.

Earlier in the day, outside in the drizzle, I had been squinting up at a dense network of pipes and supports when I realized with a jolt that I was standing where the artist Charles Sheeler had drawn one of his Rouge-inspired masterpieces, *Ballet Mechanique*, 60-plus years ago, when the Rouge symbolized the hopes and values of our society. The power of the forms is still there (even if some of the steel is rusting and vines encircle the stanchions), but the power of the idea is past, found today, I suppose, in the "clean" rooms of the Silicon Valley. Nonetheless, the Rouge remains exciting, even thrilling; for now, it is one of those rare American places where a heroic past is linked to a vital present.

Last spring, BMW was featured at the Amelia Island Concours, and among the cars they brought were the 1975 Sebring winner and the CSL that had been painted by Alexander Calder. I had raced both, and it felt like a reunion.

BMW had arranged a photo shoot, and in the morning cold the bright colors of the Calder car seemed to give off heat. Cars are inanimate objects, but with five or six of us grouped around Calder's bright yellows and reds, it was as if the artist himself was nearby.

BMW Calder Art Car
ROAD & TRACK, MARCH 2014

t was the summer of 1975, and the BMW factory team was barnstorming across America, its fast and beautiful 3.0 CSLs the center of attention at every race. I had been chosen to be the token American on this elite squad, which included Hans Stuck, Ronnie Peterson, and Brian Redman. (David Hobbs eventually joined BMW, after the driving standards were lowered.) But it was a Frenchman virtually unknown to the racing world who drove for the team under highly unusual circumstances that history will remember—not for his driving, but for an idea that still resonates today. His name was Hervé Poulain.

Hervé was an amateur racer with a dream of running Le Mans. Through his work as an auctioneer he had befriended Alexander Calder, the inventor of the mobile and a mythic figure in the art world. Calder had recently given Braniff's planes a new look, and Hervé asked him if he would do a car—and the artist agreed. Hervé's plan was to trade the Calder paint job for a ride.

Brimming with confidence, he went first to Renault. They turned him down cold. Next, he tried Lola, and they, too, said no. Hervé was an emotional guy, and these two rejections plunged him into despair. His next move made no sense at all, and he has never been able to explain what led him to BMW. Somehow it had escaped him that their team was in the States, and that they didn't even have an entry for Le Mans.

But luck was with the Frenchman. The day he arrived in Munich, team boss Jochen Neerpasch was having a rare day in his office. Better still, he knew Calder's work and liked it. Suddenly, Jochen had an idea. Why not insure the CSL—not for its value as a racing car, but as an *art object*. He was known for being conservative; this would stir things up.

He went straight to Lloyd's, and the venerable old company drew up a policy for one million dollars. A million bucks! You could almost hear the publicity machine whirring. What was the car really worth? Who knew? And what would it look like? Neerpasch worried that the BMW executives might not accept anything that interfered with the engineering-pure lines of their cars. Instead, the top brass endorsed the project; seeing a CSL through the eyes of a famous artist seemed to be worthwhile, even if nobody knew in what way.

A three-foot-long model, pure white, was dispatched to Calder, who was American, with a studio in France. He was 76 and had little more than a year to live, but his paint scheme was as gay and cheerful as a child's toy. The design was asymmetrical, the various shapes appearing to be arbitrary, as if the whole thing had only taken a few minutes.

Back in Munich, BMW technicians transferred the design from the model to the race car, and it looked terrific! Calder had used only primary colors, plus white. The paint had barely dried when the car was exhibited at Munich's Haus der Kunst, where it was right at home with the best paintings.

Neerpasch, knowing that I was an artist, had kept me involved as the project progressed, so I wasn't surprised when he offered me the ride. It meant missing an IMSA race in which I would have been driving with Brian Redman—a sure win—but the lure of Le Mans was too great, and I flew to France. The team was staying in a centuries-old chateau, and the car was being prepared in a picturesque stone barn.

I hadn't been there long before I sensed an odd lack of urgency, and it turned out that several components—redesigned in the newer cars—were almost certain to fail. In fact, plans had already been made for dinner—on Saturday night, when the race would still be in the early stages. As for having Hervé take a turn at the wheel, why not? If he screwed up, there really wasn't anything to lose. At the last minute, Jochen made a classy move by signing Jean Guichet, a grand gentleman who had won Le Mans in 1964. But in a sense, the racing was incidental. The program had been declared a success before we even did a lap. The chemistry was just right: the million-dollar policy, the debate about whether the car was art or not, the great way it looked, the glamour of Le Mans. Editors across Europe were inspired to run stories in the lifestyle section of their papers. It would later be claimed that the Art Car, as it was becoming known, got more ink than the winner of the race.

Bill Warner commissioned this article for his Amelia Island extravaganza. BMW brought the Calder Art Car, which I had driven at Le Mans in 1975, and Bill featured it in his program.

That year, the qualifying sessions ended at midnight, and as time was running out, our engineer noticed that the temperature was dropping abnormally fast. This was before the chicanes, and the Mulsanne straight was three miles where horsepower-boosting cooler air would be worth several seconds a lap. Suddenly, the whole attitude of the team changed. Fresh tires went on, and Neerpasch motioned for me to get in the car. Jochen was a distinguished former driver and a very low-key guy. I don't remember if he gave me any instructions; it was obvious to all of us that a fast lap—a really fast lap—would bring us a moment of glory that had nothing to do with our famous paint job.

The track was nearly deserted. I completed the warm-up lap with everything looking good. Now for the one that would count. I got through the Esses and as I came out of Tertre Rouge, I saw very bright headlights close behind me. A moment later a prototype came by not going much faster than I was. A drafting partner? I tucked in behind him, and on my fourth-to-fifth upshift, I went way past the red line. I had to stay with this guy!

The CSLs looked boxy, but they were always very fast in a straight line. Earlier in the year, Hans Stuck and I had led the Daytona 24 Hours with ease, and the car had been fastest at Sebring, too. Now here I was, inches behind a prototype, which was so low I could barely see it over the hood. I stopped looking at the tach. I knew they built great engines at BMW, and I could only hope this was one of them.

We neared the end of the straight, and with my much heavier car I had to brake earlier for the slow Mulsanne Corner than he did. In seconds, he was through the turn and gone. Now I was alone on the road, with the rest of the lap to complete.

Four years earlier I had held the absolute record for a few hours, my NART Ferrari 512 M just consuming the track, a rare condition where the faster you go, the easier it gets. The Bimmer just flew through the rest of the lap.

Our time—meaningless today, but etched in my mind—was 4:06.0, and it astonished everyone. It put us 10th on the grid, and when the cars were all lined up, there was our big, bright box sitting on a carpet of low prototypes. BMW had flown Calder to the track for the start, and anyone with a camera wanted a shot of him with the car. He was wearing his studio clothes—L.L. Bean shirt, paint-splattered pants—and looked like the authentic artist that he was. He'd had some drinks, and I don't think he really grasped why he was there, or what was going on. But he was the center of attention, and I think he liked that. The consensus was that we wouldn't last more than six hours, so while everyone else was conserving their cars for the long grind ahead, I was blasting gleefully along. Some lap charts had us running as high as sixth. In a sedan!

I had expected the engine to go, but it was the driveshaft, on lap 73, just as night was coming on. Hervé had driven carefully with no mishaps, and when I last saw him, he was in the team's motor home, despairing our early retirement and looking like Socrates about to drink his hemlock. But he was being consoled by two lovely women, so I assumed that things would soon be looking up.

Hervé had really started something.

BMW ran an Art Car in the next three Le Mans. In 1976, Frank Stella countered Calder's colorful exuberance with a black-and-white graph-paper grid—rational and elegant. Roy Lichtenstein used his hard-edged comic-book vocabulary, while Andy Warhol painted the car by hand right in the middle of a party.

So are these cars art? Absolutely. The artists encountered all the same ups and downs you encounter any time you make art. They took it very seriously; these were clearly going to be very high-profile, and they didn't want to look bad. Artists are competitive, too. The first one was the easiest; nothing to compare it to. Calder simply adapted the shapes and colors he was used to working with every day. He didn't have to invent anything, and his vocabulary was ideally suited to the assignment.

In one sense, the first four Art Cars have little to do with racing. The Calder car ran only that one time, and retired to traveling the world as a glamorous exhibit. But looked at another way, I believe the cars are right there at the heart of the sport—that in a very special and intelligent way, they have broadened the scope of what cars can look like, something that fascinates us all. *"Wind, sand, and cars" is obviously a rip-off of Antoine de Saint-Exupéry's classic Wind, Sand, and Stars. Most viewers will get it, and—I hope—be amused.*

The second paragraph ends with "Red cars, dominant in the desert." The repeated heavy-thudding Ds are great to read when I'm doing the voice-over. Here, in print, they look foolish. But it seems I had Ds on the brain; four of them ("day is done" and "decision in the desert") anchor the last two lines.

Bahrain '09

Wind, sand, and cars . . . quick cars, racing across the dunes in the kingdom of Bahrain.

The country is governed by a constitutional monarchy, while the track has been ruled in recent times by Ferrari—red cars, dominant in the desert.

But now Ferrari is in trouble . . . their cars are slow and fragile, their team tactics born of desperation.

And they are not alone in the gloom: Renault and McLaren—kings of the sport—are mired in the midfield murk . . . and BMW is a nightmare of unrealized promise. Three teams smoldering with the desire to get back on top.

The new rulers are the princes of F1: Brawn, with a car white as the desert, its body sculpted like a dune . . . and Red Bull, with a machine devised by a genius and driven by the hottest in the business.

Who will wear the crown when the day is done?

Find out now; the Grand Prix of Bahrain, the decision in the desert is . . . *next!*

This was my second article commissioned by Larry Webster, *Road & Track*'s new editor. I was a dissident voice in an issue celebrating Porsche's 50th anniversary.

R & T has always been loyal to Porsche—excessively. You'd think no one else made cars. As Porsche's 50th anniversary approached, I could hear the keening of the sycophants, months before the Sacred Porsche Issue went to print. Views at Variance—I had a few things I wanted to point out; for example, their flagship model, the 911, has the engine in the wrong place. And so on.

The Loyal Opposition
ROAD & TRACK, MAY 2013

Porsche—revered by its legions of owners, feared by its competitors, a deified name in the world of cars, a company that in the minds of many can do no wrong. I shared this view, until the first time I actually raced a Porsche. That's when things began to go downhill.

The race was the 24 Hours of Daytona, 1966. I was driving my newly acquired 904, which the factory itself had prepared. It was also running 904s, and we were to be an unofficial part of the team, trading technical info and so forth. Before practice, we received a visit from the team manager, the famed Huschke von Hanstein, who was kindly and avuncular, repeating the factory's promise of full cooperation. But then practice began, and the unexpected happened: We were faster than the factory cars. I expected congratulations from my new buddy Huschke, but we never saw him again. Lesson learned: Beating the factory was strictly verboten.

Later that year, I sold the 904—the first and only Porsche I've ever owned—and fate has punished me, repeatedly, for being disloyal. As everyone knows, 904s combine great design with scarcity, and today they're worth . . . Don't tell me. I know I let a fortune slip through my hands. Lesson number two: Never sell a Porsche. There is a department right there in the factory known simply as Revenge. People go in there but never come back out.

My next Porsche encounter furthered my education. It was at Sebring, 1967, a Trans-Am drive with Peter Gregg in his 911. We won in spite of the car, not because of it. Production of the 911 had begun three years earlier, so I expected the car to be fully sorted. Instead, it handled terribly. The front end darted from side to side as if it had massive toe-out, while at the rear, the engine swung things around like a pendulum run amok. First gear, required for Sebring's ultratight hairpin, was hidden off by itself somewhere under your thigh, and there was no shift gate, which left you stirring the lever, hoping that it might encounter a gear by luck.

But the 911 was beautifully turned out, and the engine was so obviously powerful that it was just assumed the whole car was great. In fact, it was Peter's talent and Jack Atkinson's careful prep that flattered the car and helped give it a reputation it really didn't deserve.

In fact, teams that ran Porsches in those years often improved the cars, with no help from the factory, turning losers into winners. When Tony Adamowicz won 6 out of 10 Trans-Am races in a row in 1968, his 911 was what he called a "California hot rod," with a suspension built by the brilliant Mac Tilton. The early 917s were virtually undrivable until John Horsman redesigned the tail. And, most famously, Mark Donohue managed to transform the prototype Can-Am car from a problem-ridden flop into a 1,500hp monster so fast that it ruined the Can-Am. Nobody could compete with it.

The 911 was bad; the 917 was worse. Porsche introduced it in 1969, and the favorable first impression it made—leading Le Mans—proved totally misleading, the utterly fearless Vic Elford having driven it as no other man could. Those first cars were desperately crude. Brian Redman told me his would change lanes without warning at 235 mph, and I remember Pedro Rodríguez passing me on the Mulsanne, white as a sheet and steering like mad on a wide, dead-straight part of the track. Sticking out beyond the front axles, the driver's feet were completely unprotected. Welds cracked in the space-frame chassis. Porsche had rushed construction of the 917s, building 25 of them to comply with an FIA homologation requirement. Hindsight says they never should have sold one to an inexperienced privateer, but they did, to English amateur John Woolfe, and he was killed on the first lap.

For 1970, Porsche had refined their car, now designated the 917K, and it had seven entered. These cars were sledgehammers, and they were built when Porsche, after years of dominating the smaller classes, was finally going for the overall win. But Ferrari also wanted Le Mans, and it was out in force, looking to regain the luster of earlier years. The North American Racing Team had a new 512 S for Ronnie Bucknum and me.

In those days, you were either a Porsche man or a Ferrari man, and team spirit was very much alive. When I'd glance down at the steering wheel and see the Prancing Horse, it never failed to give me a thrill. We finished fourth, behind three Porsches, and the next year we were third, again beaten only by Porsches. A fourth and a third, each time the highest-placed Ferrari. Wasn't that something to be proud of? Maybe. But all I could do was curse the cars that had beaten us.

For the good of the sport, wouldn't a Ferrari (mine) have looked better in the winner's circle? I certainly think so, and always remember, *De gustibus non est disputandum.* (In matters of taste, there can be no disputes.) Besides, Porsche would go on to win 15 more times at Le Mans, including seven in a row. Couldn't it have delayed the onslaught by one lousy year?

The sting of those defeats has faded over time to a dull ache that flares up when somebody starts talking about those "legendary" 917s. Having a shot at Le Mans and missing is something that can haunt you the rest of your life. Just ask David Hobbs. Or Brian Redman. It's not exactly Porsche's fault that I never won Le Mans, but the loss took a lot of free-floating negative vibes and focused them into envy and resentment.

Porsche's success resonated strongly in the United States, important because half of its cars were bought by Americans. Emboldened by the company's successes, Porsche owners now brazenly disdained all other makes. I would speak at a Porsche Club meeting and any story that didn't have me driving a Porsche caused the members to grow restive. By the end of the evening, when conversation invariably narrowed to a discussion of obscure details of their cars, it was all too obvious that I was not, and would never be, one of the true brotherhood.

The automotive press, too, bought into the Zuffenhausen mystique, heaping praise on everything Porsche. Even *Road & Track*, usually the paragon of editorial integrity, swooned at each tiny change to the 911. Criticism of this car was seemingly off-limits. Ah, the 911. Worshipped. Iconic. Stupid.

Dig back to its beginnings, and you find yourself in Nazi Germany with a lot of things going on that are best left in the swirling Wagnerian mists. What emerges is the VW Beetle, a superb design for cheap transportation, but wholly unsuited as the basis for anything with sporting aspirations. The engine, you see, was in the wrong place—so far out back that there was nothing beyond it except a license plate and exhaust fumes, and where its weight, when acted upon by even the slightest cornering force, swung the tail out to every ditch and guardrail. Since time began, each iteration of the 911 has started life handicapped by this flawed DNA, and many of the highly touted improvements were little more than steps toward making the 911 less bad.

Stuttgart's engineers knew all this, of course, and in the late 1970s, they managed to get front-engine sports cars, free of the 911's baggage, into production. These were excellent cars, but by the time they arrived, it was too late; the 911 had gained real traction in the marketplace. Management shifted the company's development focus back to the 911. The story goes that the decision was made quickly by the two top men, and it was seminal, creating a blueprint for the company's future.

These people had their eyes wide open. They knew that no matter how much you refined the 911, you'd still have something less than optimum. But they were able to look beyond that and appreciate what they did have: a unique product that had stood the test of time. Porsche was able to take all the hard-earned knowledge acquired through the years and turn liabilities into strengths. You hear about how people who survived crippling illnesses in childhood grow up to be stars. The 911 is that kind of story.

Last fall, my son John and I were in the paddock at Lime Rock when we spotted a 911 Turbo S. John doesn't carry the Porsche baggage that I do, and he found the car stunning. To my surprise, I soon agreed with him. The Turbo combined grace and poise with a muscular look, and its performance numbers were well past the threshold of sanity: 530hp and a top speed of almost 200 mph. Sure, its basic lines dated back to the Pleistocene epoch, but I found this comforting—evidence that stubborn perseverance can pay off. Suddenly, this car made other manufacturers seem to be lurching from one style to another in search of something Porsche already had, a kind of gravitas that only time (and a few 917s) can give you.

Alone among major manufacturers, Porsche has stuck with the idea that cars don't always have to be new, but they do have to be better—and today it fields a lineup like nobody else's.

R & T *liked to think of itself as an automotive* New Yorker. *Grammatical errors and typos were rare, thanks to eagle-eyed proofreader Ellida Maki. Humor was part of the mission statement. Much of it was subtle—an unexpected turn of phrase. There were some cartoons, Stan Mott illustrated the adventures of the Cyclops racing team (a real Cyclops was displayed in the lobby), and the back page was devoted to a photo with a funny caption. (Two men are looking into a ditch at a wrecked car. "Good tires," says one, "not great tires.")*

In the April Fools' road tests an unlikely vehicle was subjected to the same performance tests of a car. Needless to say, these assignments were highly coveted, and I have Tom Bryant to thank for giving me more than my fair share. I tested a bobsled, an Iditarod sled-dog team, my uncle's wind-driven contraption (see Wind Wagon, April 2004, page 31), and, here, a steam engine.

1924 Baldwin Decapod
ROAD & TRACK, APRIL 2003

Much of a steam locomotive's appeal lies in its excesses: the huge boiler, the thrashing pistons, the smoke, the immense black weight perched delicately on the narrow rails. There is also the mystery of what it must be like to ride in one, an experience usually reserved for those Promethean figures seen leaning out of the cab, calmly squinting through the steam as they rush by, headed for the horizon.

From Julius Caesar to Andrew Jackson, travel had been at the same rate; it took the locomotive to introduce the idea of speed. Owing its existence to a simple yet extraordinary fact of physics (water heated into steam expands in volume 1,600 times), the locomotive was itself a force for expansion as our population moved westward in the second half of the 19th century. The long, mournful whistle of a train beckoned generations of Americans to leave home and seek their destiny.

Then, suddenly, around 1955, steam engines were gone. Like dinosaurs, they were victims of their own specialization. Most had been custom-built in small quantities to meet the specific needs of the railroads that purchased them. (In 1910 one of the leading manufacturers listed more than 500 models.) Built of steel and iron, running on fire and water, steam locomotives were brutish, elemental machines—but they were also prima donnas, requiring parts that were hard to get, intense maintenance by expert crews, and special facilities such as turntables, roundhouses, water tanks, and coaling stations. They were replaced by diesels, which were anonymous, mass-produced machines that made up in efficiency what they lacked in character.

Today it is impossible to see a steam locomotive other than through the lens of nostalgia—and yet a few still exist in operating condition. There are about 40 or so tourist lines that run steam, including the well-known Durango to Silverton Railroad in Colorado. But when I succeeded in interesting editor in chief Tom Bryant in a track test ("It corners on rails!" "It can smoke anything!"), the place I knew I wanted to go was the Strasburg Rail Road, a popular attraction in southeastern Pennsylvania. It's run by Linn Moedinger, a second-generation railroader who knows almost all there is to know about steam engines. Plus, I had fallen in love with Strasburg's No. 90, a handsomely proportioned locomotive that Linn promised I could drive.

No. 90 was built in 1924 by the Baldwin Locomotive Works as a freight locomotive, which meant that it had high tractive force (it can pull 1,000 tons, about 20 cars) but a low top speed (less than 55 mph). Passenger locomotives, by contrast, have relatively low tractive force but high top speed. No. 90 hauled sugar beets in northern Colorado for the Great Western Rail Road until 1967, which made it one of the last steamers running in the United States. Instead of being scrapped, No. 90 was bought by the Strasburg Rail Road for the grand sum of $36,552, spares included. (Linn puts its current value at more than $1 million.) Lovingly maintained, it has spent the last 35 years being admired and photographed as it pulls trains loaded with tourists along the Strasburg's main line. This is one engine that got lucky.

The first I saw of No. 90 was just its smoke, drifting like an exhaled breath out of the tall chimney stack of the engine house. It was right after dawn. This was in Amish country, with sprawling fields of iridescent green maize, white barns, horse-drawn buggies, and towns with curious names such as Paradise and Bird-in-Hand.

Inside the engine house, 23-year-old Chuck Trusdell (a "hostler," in railroad speak) was getting the locomotive ready. This was a two-hour process that included greasing 58 separate fittings, topping up the tender (capacity: 15 tons of bituminous coal, 9,000 gallons of water), and stoking the fire in the firebox. Even just sitting still, No. 90 was about as close to a living thing as a machine can get. It made heavy sounds, panting and wheezing. It rattled. Water ran down its sides, beading like necklaces on the hot, oily metal. Small tongues of flame fell from the firebox. The air brake muttered—*latch, thunk*—and steam seeped from a dozen valves and fissures. As the boiler pressure climbed slowly from its overnight "resting" pressure of 80 psi to its operating pressure of 200 psi, the locomotive seemed to swell, radiating waves of heat.

"As the pressure comes up, it changes from a puppy to a beast," Chuck told me as he backed the locomotive out of the engine house into the yard. *Road & Track*'s Joe Rusz (armed with cameras and soaked with sweat) and I were with him up in the cab, the floor of which was about eight feet off the ground. Two narrow seats, one by each window, did not promise long-term comfort—or safety. There were no seat belts in sight, and Linn had said, "If there's trouble, join the birds!" That is, jump. (Shades of Masten Gregory.)

Ominously, there was no way to steer. The heating system, however, was as good as it gets. A foot pedal actuated jawlike doors, which opened to the firebox, where things were a cozy 2,500 degrees. With each *chuff!* the coals leapt up, reacting to the outdraft of air from the top of the firebox. As for the controls and instrumentation, the array of dials, levers, and valves at the front of the cab looked like the work of a baroque plumber gone berserk.

By now the sun was up, and the platform was filling with people who had bought tickets for the first trip of the day. Chuck turned No. 90 over to the engineer, Dr. Andy Sellers (in his spare time, he's a surgeon), and his fireman, Al Hornman. At 11:00 a.m. sharp, with the bell clanging and the whistle shrieking, we set off for Paradise.

A steam locomotive works by using fire to heat water, and the resulting steam sets in motion pistons and connecting rods, which turn the wheels. The mechanical stuff is pretty basic, but the steam is another story. The steam is protean, changing its form again and again. First, it's heated in the boiler; then, it's run through what is called a superheater, which raises its temperature to as much as 600 degrees Fahrenheit, while at the same time drying it out. At atmospheric pressure (14.7 psi), steam, as already noted, occupies 1,600 times the volume of water at the same temperature. But the boiler, like a car radiator, is pressurized (to more than 200 psi), so the steam enters the cylinder in highly compacted form. The piston begins to move, and the area for the steam to occupy increases. The pressure drops back toward 14.7 psi as the steam expands—violently.

That violence is part of the aura of every steam locomotive, and you could feel it up in the cab. It was loud, sooty, and intensely hot. And busy: Andy and Al worked without a break, shoveling coal, blowing the whistle for the level crossings, watching the temperatures and pressures, fine-tuning the amount of steam being fed to the cylinders. As the big connecting rods, 500 pounds apiece, drove the wheels, thrusting first on one side, then the other, No. 90 slammed back and forth on the rails, like a horse shaking its head; only the wheel flanges kept us from being thrown off the tracks. (Passenger locomotives would typically have lighter rods, a shorter stroke, very precise counterbalancing of all the moving parts, and much bigger wheels. No. 90's wheels are 56 inches in diameter. The world record for steam locomotives, 126 mph, was set by an engine with 80-inch driving wheels.)

With the rails less than 5 feet apart, and the cab 10 feet wide, I was actually sitting cantilevered out beyond the tracks—an unnerving feeling, one that reminded me of being in a tree house in a high wind. Plus it was odd, as the passenger, to be sitting in the left seat. (It is an unexplained part of railroad culture that American engineers sit on the right and English engineers sit on the left.) Outward vision to the side was excellent, but the view up the tracks was blocked by the long barrel of the boiler. Was not being able to see where we were going disconcerting? Hey, No. 90, with its tender, weighs 185 tons. If we hit something, we would win.

Fuel economy was not good. For every 20 miles, we were consuming roughly a ton of coal (that's a lot of shoveling!) and 1,700 gallons of water. The water limited us to a cruising range of little more than 100 miles—and you don't take chances with water. Low water leads to boiler explosions. Compared with collisions and derailments, boiler explosions are relatively rare, but they are shatteringly violent, and usually kill both engineer and fireman.

At first glance, you might think No. 90's designers at Baldwin had omitted suspension altogether—and certainly the rough, lurching ride would do little to change your mind. In fact, small but exceptionally stiff leaf springs (loading is 17 tons per axle, and the total travel is only three inches), positioned longitudinally along the top of the frame, redistribute the weight on the driving wheels as they encounter dips and rises. The springs are connected by what are called equalizer bars, which transfer weight along from one wheel to another, much as anti-rollbars do in racing cars. This arrangement permits a tiny amount of roll in the corners, but it's more than offset by the banking of the turns—what railroaders call "superelevation"—so locomotives always appear to be leaning into the corners.

The springs also act as shock absorbers, damping jolts that would otherwise be transmitted directly to the frame, and because they act to keep the wheels in contact with the rails, traction is improved. This is important when you are trying to pull a heavy train, and all you have are four-inch-wide steel wheels on steel rails (which are crowned, so each contact patch is the size of a dime).

Wheelspin is common, especially when the rails are wet, so locomotives are fitted with a kind of traction control that could have saved millions if Bernie had mandated it for Formula One. Sand is released from a small pipe directly in front of the driving wheels. Racing should also consider No. 90's "tires," which are bands of steel that are heated, then shrunk onto the outer circumference of the wheels. You could forget about pit stops; these babies last over 250,000 miles. The brakes are shoes that press against the outside of the steel tires. You can easily lock up the wheels, but with the lousy coefficient of friction and the enormous weight, don't count on stopping anytime soon.

At the end of the day, Joe Rusz and I had dinner with Linn and his wife, Susan, who runs the railroad's bookstore and souvenir shops, an operation that, including the railroad itself, employs 80 people. Susan and Linn live in a historic brick house, nearly 300 years old, that they have restored.

Preservation seems to come naturally to this family. In 1958, it was Linn's dad who rescued the Strasburg when petitions of abandonment had been filed. Linn served an apprenticeship under a Pennsylvania Railroad boilermaker, and he belongs to the last generation of railroaders that have been taught by men who actually ran steam engines in their heyday. Like those who are keeping alive the techniques of wooden boat construction, he is aware that any knowledge he doesn't record is at risk of being lost. "From here on," he says, "it will all be secondhand."

The next morning Linn sent me out to drive No. 90. Chuck steamed down the main line to a suitable stretch, brought the locomotive to a halt, and motioned for me to take over. I wished to step up to the controls with a sense of authority, but there were no familiar rituals for me to enact. No belts to fasten. No engine to start. No steering wheel to give me somewhere to put my hands.

Latch, thunk went the air brake. Steam drifted past the window and out above the maize. The big 10-inch dial read 200; the boiler pressure was up; the "beast" was ready to go. A car, I realized, has to be urged into action by being revved up; only then will it produce the power it needs to get going. No. 90, by contrast, had the power; that 600-degree superheated steam was just waiting to be released.

The time had come. I reached for the whistle cord and gave it one pull and then another, signaling my intentions to some bemused Holsteins.

Next, following Chuck's instructions, I began pushing and pulling levers, closing the cylinder cocks and releasing the brakes. Then, with my left hand, I reached for the throttle bar. It's as long as a baseball bat, as if the power on tap requires something proportionally big to unleash it. I pulled the bar back a few notches—cautiously, because Chuck said I would get wheelspin if I let too much steam into the cylinders. After a moment's hesitation, as if a turbo was spooling up, the steam reached the pistons and we were under way. This was not a surge of acceleration; it was instead the most sublime sort of movement, which is the effortless overcoming of enormous weight. Our 185 tons—more than 250 F1 cars—was moving down the rails, gathering speed.

I had, of course, felt No. 90 start before, but now, with my hand on the throttle, my elbow resting on the windowsill, and my eyes scanning the track ahead, I understood the lines of sight and the leverage points that only the engineer can experience—and I realized immediately that the feeling could be addictive. To command the movement of that much machine was serious business, and yet I felt a little giddy because a childhood fantasy was at last coming true. Look, Ma, that's me driving!

Chuck shoveled coal into the firebox, and the heat flared back across the cab. I realized I wanted to settle in for a good, hard run down the main line, highballing through the day and into the night, racing against the clock, "scorching the ballast" and pushing our luck on the turns.

This euphoria lasted about 300 yards. Something in the fine print of Linn's insurance said I couldn't drive through level crossings, and here was one just ahead. I seized the brake and brought us to a stop. I made a few more runs, back and forth, beginning to feel comfortable with the controls. Then I reluctantly resumed my seat on the passenger side, and Chuck took us back to the station.

A small crowd had formed to watch No. 90's arrival. People waved. The day before, riding with Andy and Al, I had thought it unseemly to wave back—I hadn't earned the right. Now I did wave, albeit discreetly.

The Age of Steam is over, but the thrill of steam is very much alive.

About the Author

Sam Posey's 20-year racing career includes drives in the Indy 500 (fifth), the US Grand Prix, and the 24 Hours of Le Mans (third). In 1975 he won the 12 Hours of Sebring.

As a writer Sam has published *The Mudge Pond Express, an autobiography* (G. P. Putnam's Sons, 1975), *Playing with Trains, the story of building a train layout with his son John* (Random House, 2004), and myriad articles for *the New York Times, Reader's Digest, Sports Illustrated*, and *Road & Track*.

He has also been a well-respected TV commentator, winning the Emmy for Best Writing in Sports in 1990. Sam worked 24 years with ABC Sports, followed by 10 years with Speedvision, and is now in his third year with NBC Sports.

A Rhode Island School of Design graduate, Sam is an accomplished artist. His prints are in the permanent collections of the Tate Gallery (London) and the Walker Art Center (Minneapolis). He has also designed 45 houses, a school, a firehouse, and the Start/Finish Tower at Lime Rock.

Epilogue

My racing career has a nice symmetry to it, beginning and ending at Lime Rock. The track is a 10-minute drive from my house; imagine how lucky I am, to have one of the world's greatest tracks virtually in my backyard. Some days when the cloud layer is just right, we can hear cars shifting up as they leave the pits.

I've been racing at Lime Rock for more than 50 years, and it has changed very little; it's been a constant against which I can see changes in myself. In the midst of my career, when I was racing every week, I had little time for reflection. But now it seems more natural to explore the past, particularly when the past has so many great memories to savor.

I retired in 1982, and I assumed my track days were over. But when Skip Barber, the track's owner, created the Lime Rock Drivers' Club, he gave a membership to me and my family, and it was like a second wind. I bought a Formula Ford, which Don Breslauer has modified into a sort of Lime Rock special, a car that wouldn't be legal in any SCCA class, but is a perfect machine for this track.

The last time I took the Ford out, however, I made several mistakes that recalled ones I made in those long-ago days when I was just getting started. On top of that, I was slow. Dan Gurney once pointed out to me that somewhere between 50 and 90 you're going to slow down. I have Parkinson's, I'm 70, and what had been distant thunder is growing dismayingly close. Just as years ago a big crash at Lime Rock had shocked me into realizing just how dangerous racing can be, now these mistakes were a sign that the track has become too fast and too subtle for me.

The material in this book covers the story of my racing, in bits and pieces. It is also about my life outside racing, and putting it together has given me a chance to look back on both from a fresh point of view. Years ago, after a long dinner during which the conversation touched on many subjects, Peter Revson turned to me and said, "Sam, you think too much." He meant my interests in painting, writing, and design were distractions from my driving. He was right. Peter, and the drivers who appear in the profile section of this book, had the focus and commitment that I lacked, and they have earned their glory.

I have never felt jealous, and I would never look back and say I was anything but lucky, both in the car and outside of it.